THE
JUSTICE
MISSION

THE JUSTICE MISSION

**A VIDEO-ENHANCED
CURRICULUM REFLECTING
THE HEART OF GOD
FOR THE OPPRESSED OF
THE WORLD**

JIM HANCOCK

AND THE
INTERNATIONAL JUSTICE MISSION

International Justice Mission

The Justice Mission: A Video-Enhanced Curriculum Reflecting the Heart of God for the Oppressed of the World

Copyright © 2002 by Youth Specialties

Youth Specialties Books, 300 S. Pierce St., El Cajon, CA 92020, are published by Zondervan Publishing House, 5300 Patterson Ave. S.E., Grand Rapids, MI 49530.

Library of Congress Cataloging-in-Publication Data
Hancock, Jim, 1954-
   The Justice Mission: A Video-Enhanced Curriculum Reflecting the Heart of God for the Oppressed of the World/Jim Hancock
      p. cm.
   ISBN 0-310-24377-7
   1. Church group work with youth—Justice. 2. Justice—Study and teaching
   work. I. II. Title.

BV4447 .D43 2002
259'.23'0208—dc21

2001046834

Web site addresses listed in this book were current at the time of publication. Please contact Youth Specialties via e-mail (YS@YouthSpecialties.com) to report URLs that are no longer operational and replacement URLs if available.

All worksheets and journal pages are available to you for downloading, free of charge in several formats, to fit your needs. Go to www.YouthSpecialties.com/store/justice, and click the lesson chapter you would like. (We welcome your feedback!)

Edited by Rick Marschall
Cover and interior design by Mark Arnold
Photography provided by Ted Haddock and The International Justice Mission
Editorial and production assistance by Sarah Sheerin and Roni Valerio-Meek

Printed in the United States of America

02 03 04 05 06 07 / PC / 10 9 8 7 6 5 4 3 2 1

TABLE OF CONTENTS

ICONS/LEGENDS

The Introduction explains the foundation of this project, the Justice Mission; the purpose of this Leader's Guide; and the way we present the main points – for teaching, for internalizing, for action – in the context of youth groups. Many cited examples are from history (Bible times to recent headlines) and worldwide settings. But we pray that students not only adopt a passion for righting wrongs abroad and in broader contexts... but also to have a heart for the oppressed and neglected in their schools and neighborhoods too.

Every chapter is salted with worksheets. You have permission to photocopy these in connection with the use of these lessons in youth-group settings. In addition, all of these are available on the Youth Specialties website www.youthspecialties.com/store/justice

Every chapter concludes with directed Journaling pages, for students to reflect and carry those reflections (and inspirations) to your next session.

To make your preparation and leading easier, we have highlighted elements of the curriculum with icons, signs, and symbols:

Graphics – Please linger at the photos, spreads, and chapter dividers. Ponder, absorb, share them with students: these are powerful statements in themselves... mood-setters... discussion-starters!

Boxes – Throughout each chapter are points set off in boxes. These are main points, expanding the chapter's theme. Under each box are prompted texts for you; questions for the students; activities; definitions. But please: view them also as points of an outline for you to expand upon in your own way after prayer and preparation.

▍▍▍▍ –These bars represent sub-heads in an outline: new topics under the general theme. You can prepare to pause or initiate deeper discussions in these areas. Please note that these read as "script lines." You can read directly to your group or paraphrase the major points as discussion flows.

● **Bold Face Indents** –These are definitions and explanations of items in the text or the video segments.

[ ] – Bold brackets set apart Tips and Hints for you to do, or consider varying, in the course of the sessions. These are written to you.

This symbol signals clear or important discussion-starters for the group. You will compose questions of your own, but these are points we have integrated into the structure of the curriculum.

VIDEO –There are certain points in the flow of these sessions where the video clips are more appropriate than at other times. Let the organic flow of the session rule: a shorter clip might be more powerful than a long one... you might want to re-wind and show a clip again... you might want to repeat the clip at the very end of the session, after all the discussion has been digested. Keep the tape cued for the next session.

! –You won't find this symbol in the Leader's Guide. Consider it to mean "bathe your work with this curriculum in prayer!" and consider it to be on the top of every page, then do so. WE pray that God will bless your sessions.

FOREWORD

by Gary Haugen
President,
International Justice Mission

For me, The Justice Mission is an urgent personal story. It flows from what I have seen with my own eyes. It's about two discoveries that have shaken me to my core. First, it's about the stunning brutality and unspeakable oppression that people suffer in our world; but even more powerfully, it's about God's willingness to use perfectly ordinary Christians to perform genuine 21st century miracles of rescue and redemption.

In the last decade I've seen shocking things. I have sorted through the piled corpses of genocide in Africa. I have seen teenage girls held in literal dungeons of forced prostitution in India, and the children of the poor sold into slavery. I've heard children plead (to no avail) with corrupt authorities to release their parents from prisons of torture, and I've seen children without parents in South America brutalized by police just for sport.

Most of us have seen something of this ugliness in dark, vague images on the news. Sooner or later, these images come home to all of us, and at some point they descend upon our young people. The question is: What do we offer them? A remote control to change the channel? An up-tempo praise song or a useless sense of guilt?

I think we offer them the God of Justice, and the opportunity to actually do something. When we do so, we introduce them to the other half of the story in this fallen world; namely, that Jesus is building His kingdom, and that He is offering His people the opportunity to experience the miraculous joy of actually doing justice. But He doesn't grant the power in advance. He grants it as we go, in faith. And then Jesus keeps His promises:

"The Spirit of the Lord is on me, because he has anointed me to preach good news to the poor. He has sent me to proclaim freedom for the prisoners and recovery of sight for the blind, to release the oppressed, to proclaim the year of the Lord's favor." Luke 4:18-19

For those of us who have seen these glories with our own eyes, there is a yearning to tell the world. But for me, if I could share this story with just one group on the globe, it would be the Christian youth in America—for the future lies with them. Faith lies with them. And courage lies waiting within their souls, awaiting the call to a grander purpose beyond suburban safety and a gray twilight that knows no authentic victory or defeat.

This is the story that Youth Specialties has rendered so powerfully and well in The Justice Mission. Through the youth leaders who use it, this promises to be the broadest and most powerful introduction to the biblical God of Justice that the American church has ever experienced. And it does so by bringing the call of justice to the young people who will form the future of the most powerful nation on earth. The God of history is on the move, and the gates of hell shall not prevail against it.

Joyfully,

Gary A. Haugen

GOD IS BIG ON JUSTICE.
VERY BIG.

Justice is not one of those things that comes up often in Sunday School these days. But it certainly could and it certainly should. Did you know there are well over 200 mentions of justice, injustice, and oppression in the Bible? That's half as many mentions as love or salvation, but it's twice as many as money or sex (and we talk about *them* all the time!)...

Spend a little time with those 200+ passages and you'll find God is furious about oppression just about any way you look at it.

The people of God are not so furious. Oh, we're uncomfortable with oppression, indignant about injustice in the abstract, downright mad if it touches someone we know.

But many Christian churches spend way more time working on what God loves than on what God hates.

I suspect there's room for both.

> "Stop doing wrong, learn to do right! Seek justice, encourage the oppressed. Defend the cause of the fatherless, plead the case of the widow." Isaiah 1:17

I don't have to tell you that people are oppressed. We see every day how people are victimized, orphaned and widowed. The media bring us astonishing, almost instant, often reliable, frequently bloody, details of injustice from around the globe, around the clock.

The problem is—and isn't there always a problem?—most of us don't have the foggiest notion what to do about oppression.

At this moment in the long, strange history of the Church (our moment), most Christians haven't learned much about the evil of oppressors—not in Sunday School, not from the pulpit, not in the youth group. We know by observation that some individuals wreak more havoc than others. A few names come to mind...Caligula, Hitler, Stalin, Pol Pot, bin Laden... That evil is so great we can't get our arms around it. The solutions involve great wars and cultural shifts.

But evil on that scale doesn't help us understand how loan sharks, land grabbers, crooked cops and bullies—your ordinary, garden variety oppressors—work and how to stop them.

|||||
That's what The Justice Mission is about:

UNDERSTANDING HOW OPPRESSORS WORK AND HOW TO STOP THEM.

At the end of the 20th century, a group of law enforcement officers and attorneys, The International Justice Mission, emerged as an effective global instrument for extracting children from forced labor, releasing girls from prostitution, bringing murderous cops and soldiers to justice and restoring stolen land to poor farmers—all in the name of Jesus. Now they're telling the North American church what they've learned about the character and weapons of oppression, God's passion against injustice, and how to join the fight against evil. It's a good story.

The Justice Mission tells that story so your group can join the fight for justice right now and for the rest of their lives. In five sessions you'll engage your group in understanding and embracing four very big ideas:

|||||
How oppressors work (and how to stop them).

|||||
How much God hates oppression (and how to hate what God hates).

|||||
How to answer God's call to fight injustice (beginning where they are).

|||||
How to trust God's resources (doing God's work, God's way).

At the end of the process you'll guide your group in specific, sustainable action steps that create justice by overcoming oppressors.

> **Beyond summer mission trips, beyond child sponsorship, beyond personal piety, <u>The Justice Mission</u> is the next step in doing what Jesus would do.**

HOW THIS PACKAGE WORKS

One model for teaching is a content- or teacher-centered process of telling kids what they should know. This book will not follow that model.

You may be used to having curricula push you around, tell you what to do and how to do it and what the correct answer is and how long you should budget before moving to the next thing. This book is not based on that model, either.

The Justice Mission is **stimulus and response learning** based on short, **thought-provoking** videos, brainstorms, ideas, surveys, and questions. Every stimulus invites private reflection and writing or group discussion.

This is what educators call the **Socratic method**, based on Socrates' method of encouraging students to learn by asking questions. It's easy to make a case that this is the way Jesus taught: asking more questions than he answered; keeping his monologues brief, challenging, and sometimes puzzling. And did we mention brief? His longest recorded monologue, the famous "Sermon on the Mount," runs fewer than 2500 English words. It takes about five and a half minutes to speak 2500 words, not counting standing ovations. I've read the Sermon on the Mount; I don't think there were any ovations.

We do it this way because we're convinced that putting together a series of experiences and guiding kids to considered responses enables them to *learn* more than anyone is able to *teach*.

In fact, this form gets the teacher off the hook. You don't have to be an expert in oppression to help kids learn how to create justice on the earth. The Justice Mission is designed to help you learn together!

the Socratic Method
"We could lecture students about legal reasoning, but those of us who use the Socratic method prefer to foster as much active learning as possible. Just as a professor who immediately answers her students' questions loses an opportunity to help them discover the answers on their own, the professor who dispenses legal principles in classroom soliloquies will reduce students' opportunities to engage in independent critical thinking that can lead them to a deeper understanding." — Professor Elizabeth Garrett, University of Chicago Law School at the law school web site, www.law.uchicago.edu/prospective/headnotes/socratic.html

The Justice Mission guide provides the learning elements; you control the learning environment, deciding when to linger on a point that engages your group and when to move on to the next idea. Take as long as you need to get it right (not that you need anyone's permission to do that, but some folks feel bad when they color outside the lines. Relax: these lines are dotted).

Each session includes half a dozen distinct elements. Use them all or, if you're an expert user, choose what suits your group.

GATHERING

The gathering experiences are designed to get things warmed up as people arrive and get settled. In most cases there's more than you need to get the ball rolling, so don't feel compelled to use everything unless it's just working too well to stop.

VIDEO

There's a video-driven discussion segment for each session. The videos carry quite a bit of content and emotion.

Here's something we've learned about using video: Most individuals can't pull out all the good stuff in a video clip, but most *groups* can. That's why the discussion block following each segment is important. And it's why the questions focus more on what kids get from watching the video than on what we put there. If you give your group a little time to think, they'll come up with most of the important stuff. If they don't, that tells you what you need to work on.

OPERATING INSTRUCTIONS

Each session includes at least one learner-centered Bible study segment. Learner-centered means here what it means in the video discussions: find out what kids get from the passage before launching your own ideas.

THE BIG IDEA

The Big Idea is a brief block of instruction or guided discussion about a concept that needs expert information or a block of discussion to ensure your group zooms in on what's most important in the session. The Big Idea is the thread that holds everything together.

REFLECTION

Each session includes time and material for personal reflection. This is because people learn what they're *prepared* to learn more than what they're *supposed* to learn. By giving students space for purposeful reflection, you give the spirit of God and their own subconscious a chance to land on something long enough to decide what to do about it.

ACTION

The final segment in each session (other than praying) is determining what to do about what you've been talking about. In some cases that means taking specific action against evil. But let's face it, an hour, or even five hours, isn't enough time to say, "This is what I *learned.*" The Justice Mission is a crash course. The real learning takes place in doing. So, more often than not, **Action** means going further, digging deeper, thinking and praying harder about what to do. *Then* your students can say with confidence, "This is what I learned."

SOMETHING YOU WON'T FIND

You won't find trick questions or rhetorical questions here.

Rhetorical questions don't actually want an answer. So why ask them? (See what I did there? Using a rhetorical question to debunk rhetorical questions? This is why I get the medium dollars)

Trick questions are asked in order to make a point. They're considered safe because, obviously there's only one answer, right? Well...I'm not so sure about that. Consider the following question:

 Have you ever seen oppression—small or large—but failed to speak up?

That invites a yes or a no. But I honestly don't know what your answer might be. So I ask the follow up:

- How do you feel about that today?

The second question invites a more detailed answer that's important regardless of the answer to the first.

Of course it's possible someone may answer that second question with a single word— "bad," for example, or "fine." The follow up to that kind of response is, "Talk about that."

AS IF YOU NEEDED OUR PERMISSION

There's more than enough material here to fill an hour session...

- **too** much if your group gets revved up and really engages the learning processes.

- **too** much if you sing at the beginning or play games.

So think of the elements in The Justice Mission as a menu. Choose the ingredients that deliver a healthy meal for your group.

And season to taste.

- Some folks are very comfortable with physical movement, but some find that chaotic.

- Some groups incorporate art projects effortlessly; others find art messy and time-consuming

- Some groups need activities to keep things moving, others function best on the level of ideas.

You're the only one who knows what works best with your group.

We know kids but we don't know your kids. Are you doing this with six or 600? In the heart of the city? In the suburbs? In a small town? Is your group used to talking with each other or being talked to?

And we don't know *you*. We don't know your gifts, your skills, where in the world you've been, how long you've been where you are...

So—not that you need permission—please, adapt this till it works for your group. Even if that means taking eight weeks instead of five. Or taking the Justice Mission to summer camp and doing a session every morning. Knock yourself out. Mix and match. Take these elements and use them as only you can.

HERE'S A HAPPY THOUGHT

Some kids may engage The Justice Mission with greater passion than others. Maybe it's a heart thing—God touches their hearts with compassion for the oppressed. Maybe it's a calling—God may call them to pursue justice with their life's work.

Watch for those kids. Encourage them to go to the web site for more. Ask them to help you communicate the urgency of creating justice to their peers. Give them special assignments—outside research, interviews or book reports to the larger group, that kind of thing... Match pairs of those kids to work together, then look out! Heaven knows what they'll come up with.

Keep us posted on how it's going. Contact Youth Specialties or International Justice Mission and tell them you're beginning the series and they'll ask people to pray for you. And let us know if you're willing to help other youth workers who are behind you in the process.

THE JUSTICE MISSION 1
OPPRESSION

STUFF

● **List-making** setup for brainstorming; video playback; *The Justice Mission* video cued to *Oppression*; Personal Inventory sheets, pencils or pens.

GATHERING

● **Brainstorm:** Compile and rate a list of sources that give us information about the world.

THE BIG IDEA

● **Discussion:** Defining oppression.

● **Video-driven Discussion:** Oppression

OPERATING INSTRUCTIONS

● **Bible Study:** Isaiah 1:10-17.

REFLECTION

● **Personal Inventory:** What's most important?

ACTION

● **WebSite:** visit ijm.org/JusticeMission for more about the nature of injustice

● **Dig:** mass media survey

● **Journal:** Personal Journaling

THIS SESSION

When C.S. Lewis began explaining Christian faith to his post-Christian culture, he chose the notion of *unfairness* because everyone knows how it feels to be treated unfairly. **We've all been bullied by someone stronger.** We've all been lied to, tricked, cheated, and fleeced. And no one likes it, not a tiny bit. In a surprising twist, unfairness generates such deep resentment that many people end up doing to others what was done to them. It's impossible to find the logic behind hurting people—not because they hurt us but because **someone else** hurt us. There **is** no logic; it's unfair, but there it is.

> Oppression is unfairness taken to extremes.

IIIII

Oppressors use lies and force to take what rightly belongs to someone else. That, in a nutshell, is injustice.

> **Oppressors use deception and coercion—lies and force—to take what was never meant for them.**

Injustice is woven into the fabric of life. Open a news magazine, turn on your television; oppressors are there. In fact, most people are numb to it. Joseph Stalin, who ordered the killing of millions, is credited with the notion that the death of one person is a tragedy, but the death of thousands is a statistic. That's numbness.

Who has what it takes to look at global oppression without flinching? Not many. Not me. It's too big. I feel too small.

I suspect you feel that way too. And I think the kids we serve have grown up more or less expecting injustice; more or less accepting injustice as a statistical probability. This is a problem.

IIIII

Here's a solution. We took four American kids to meet individuals who are the victims of oppressors. Ben, Charissa, Lindsay, and Trever are eyewitnesses to injustice. While we looked over their shoulders these four looked in the eyes of a girl who was forced into prostitution when she should have been in seventh grade. They met a boy whose 10th-grade year was interrupted when he was forced out of school to roll beedi cigarettes for a loan shark. These are not statistics, they're tragedies, and there are a lot more like them.

Why India? We took Ben, Charissa, Lindsay, and Trever there because it was convenient timing. Consequently, you're seeing only what we saw. We're not saying this is the only—or even the worst—oppression in the world. We could have visited dozens of other places in India and

hundreds, if not thousands, of locations around the globe. There's no political violence in these videos, no forced relocation, no ethnic cleansing, no crooked cops, dishonest soldiers, corrupt judges, or paramilitary terrorism. We went to India for 10 days and this is what we found.

Truth be told, it hasn't been that long since all this oppression and more was common in North America. Oppression is every place. So, no finger pointing.

Except at oppressors.

Whatever they look like and wherever they live, they're the bad guys. God, who is enormously tolerant of failure, mistakes, slips, backslides, and screwups, is pointedly, passionately intolerant of oppression. That's what we want your kids to get in this session.

They already know what God loves. We want them to start thinking about what God hates.

GATHERING

Brainstorm: Compile and rate a list of sources that provide information about the world.

[ASK SOMEONE TO WRITE THE LIST ON A BOARD SO EVERYONE CAN SEE IT. PUSH YOUR GROUP TO THINK FAST AND SPEAK THEIR MINDS.]

Let's make a list of sources that give us information about the world.

IIIII
I'll go first: CNN. MSNBC. FoxNews. OK, fill out the list with other sources of information about the world. I have another one: *The Daily Show.* What other sources give us information about the world?

[WITHOUT HIJACKING THE PROCESS, KEEP PRIMING THE PUMP IF THINGS MOVE SLOWLY.]

- How about business travelers?

- What about tourists?

- Missionaries?

- Military travelers?

- Diplomats?

- Artists and storytellers?

? Let's rank this list from most to least reliable? **[ASK YOUR LIST MAKER TO NUMBER THE LIST AS THE GROUP VOTES.]**

? Do some of these sources strike you more as propaganda than reliable eyewitnesses?

IIIII
Talk about that: What do you think makes one source more reliable than another?

THE BIG IDEA

Here's a working definition of *justice:*

[THIS WOULD BE A GOOD PLACE FOR A SLIDE OR POSTER]

"Justice is working to see that every person has what is rightly hers."

? Can you improve on that definition?

Here's a working definition of oppression:

[THIS WOULD BE A GOOD PLACE FOR A SLIDE OR POSTER]

"Oppression is using force and lies to deprive others of what is rightly theirs."

? Can you improve on that definition?

? What are some things our most reliable sources tell us about justice and oppression around the world?

VIDEO: OPPRESSION

VIDEO I want to show you a short story about some people who have seen what we're talking about with their own eyes. It's called <u>Oppression</u>.

[WHEN THE VIDEO ENDS.]

? On a scale of one to five, how credible do you find these storytellers?

[IF YOU WISH TO CREATE SOME PHYSICAL MOVEMENT AT THIS POINT, HAVE THE GROUP RESPOND BY MOVING TO A PLACE IN THE ROOM THAT REPRESENTS A SCALE OF ONE TO FIVE AND COMPLETE THE SENTENCE TO EACH OTHER. OTHERWISE, ASK THEM TO RESPOND WITH A SHOW OF HANDS OR SIMPLY SPEAK UP.]

1	**2**	**3**	**4**	**5**
They're hard to believe, because...	I'd need more evidence, because ...	I'm torn, because...	I think I believe them, because...	They're easy to believe, because...

? Were there any surprises for you in their stories?

? What's the most significant thing you heard or saw in the video?

- Why do you think that's important?

? Compare what you saw and heard about oppressors with the worst bullies you ever knew at school or in your neighborhood.

- What differences do you see between ordinary bullies and oppressors?

- Have you ever been at the mercy of a bully? [*IF YES, ASK HOW THAT FELT AND HOW IT WAS RESOLVED (IF IT WAS RESOLVED).*]

? Ben says oppressors trap their victims. What do you think about that?

- What evidence did you see that supports or contradicts Ben's claim?

? Charissa thought the rock quarry was the worst thing she saw. Describe the worst thing you saw.

- Why do you think that struck you?

? Lindsay thinks the church focuses on what God loves to the exclusion of what God hates. What do you think about that?

- How can we make room for both?

? Trever says if it weren't for oppressors we could solve the problems of poverty. What do you think about that?

- What do oppressors do to make difficult circumstances impossible?

> You'll see a lot of the four American kids in The Justice Mission videos. Direct your group to ijm.org for more on who they are and what they're up to. If the question comes up during this session, here's a quick introduction:

Ben just graduated from high school where he was one of those athlete/scholars who make the rest of us feel uncoordinated and/or ignorant. Ben is on his way to college to study computer science.

Charissa recently moved to a new city, so she's still adjusting to her surroundings. After school, Charissa indulges her passion for water polo and opera (is that well-rounded or bipolar?). She just completed her sophomore year in high school.

Lindsay's parents rescued her from an orphanage in Korea (where they were told she was hopelessly autistic). Lindsay went to college on a diving scholarship. She just finished her sophomore year.

Trever is a high school senior. You may recognize him from his after school job as a Hollywood actor. But he's not acting here. Trever is on this trip because he loves Jesus and cares about people.

The other two Americans in the video are **Bob Mosier** and **Gary Haugen**.

Bob is the chief investigator for International Justice Mission, the good folks who guided us through our discovery.

Gary is the president and chief storyteller for International Justice Mission. You'll learn more about IJM as the series unfolds. If you can't wait, check out ijm.org or find Gary's book, *Good News About Injustice* from InterVarsity Press

▌▌▌▌▌
Here's a laundry list of oppression. Stand up if you know about specific examples of each injustice (in the video or wherever), sit down if you don't.
[USE THE EXPLANATIONS OR NOT AS YOU SEE FIT.]

- **abusive child labor:** depriving children of health, safety, and wholeness by forcing them to work for unfair wages or in dangerous conditions

- **child pornography:** sexualized images of children for adult gratification

- **child prostitution:** forcing children to engage in sex acts with adults

- **forced prostitution:** forcing adults to engage in sex acts against their will

- **extorting or withholding wages:** depriving workers of rightful payment

- **corrupt seizure of property:** taking property from its rightful owner by force, intimidation or dirty dealing

- **corruption of justice:** unlawful use of courts and governmental bodies

- **intimidation:** the unlawful threat of force or economic deprivation

- **abusive police** or **military actions:** unauthorized use of power by police or soldiers against law-abiding people

- **state-supported discrimination** and **abuse:** legal but unjust actions against law-abiding citizens or immigrants

- **torture:** individualized cruelty and mutilation against detained persons

- **forced migration:** unlawful eviction and relocation

- **kidnapping or detaining without lawful charge or trial:** just like it sounds

- **execution without lawful charge or trial:** assassination and other murders

- **state, rebel or paramilitary terrorism:** unlawful use of sudden force against non-military targets

- **racial or ethnic violence:** unlawful violence against persons because of racial or ethnic characteristics

> In every case of injustice, an oppressor abuses power to take what rightly belongs to someone else: his life, property, dignity, liberty, or the fruits of his legitimate effort.

 What sort of person would do that to another human being?

 Faced with all this oppression, what are we supposed to do?

② Do you think it's fair for a person to say she loves God if she doesn't love what God loves? Why?

IIIII
Let's create a quick list of things God loves—everything we can think of in three minutes:

[ASK SOMEONE TO WRITE DOWN THE LIST SO EVERYONE CAN SEE IT.]

② What makes you think God loves those things?

② The next question demands to be asked: Do you think it's fair for a person to say he loves God if he doesn't hate what God hates? Because...

IIIII
Let's make a list of things God hates. We'll take three minutes.

[ASK SOMEONE TO WRITE DOWN THE LIST SO EVERYONE CAN SEE IT.]

② What makes you think God hates those things?

OPERATING INSTRUCTIONS

Let's look at Isaiah 1:10-17.

**[HERE'S A LITTLE BACKGROUND: THE PEOPLE OF GOD WEREN'T ACTING MUCH LIKE PEOPLE OF GOD AND THEY WERE IN DEEP TROUBLE. VERSE 9 SAYS: "UNLESS THE LORD ALMIGHTY HAD LEFT US SOME SURVIVORS, WE WOULD HAVE BECOME LIKE SODOM, WE WOULD HAVE BEEN LIKE GOMORRAH." ALL GOD'S CHILDREN KNEW THE STORY OF SODOM AND GOMORRAH, TWO TOWNS WHERE THE PEOPLE WERE SO EVIL THAT GOD WIPED THEM OFF THE FACE OF THE EARTH WITH A RAIN OF FIRE.
ISAIAH PICKED UP THE PANICKY TONE IN WHAT WAS LEFT OF THE KINGDOM OF JUDAH AFTER MOST OF THE POPULATION WAS HAULED OFF TO FORCED LABOR IN ANOTHER COUNTRY. IN THE AFTERMATH, EVERYONE WAS FEELING RELIGIOUS. IN VERSE 10, GOD SPEAKS TO THE PEOPLE OF JUDAH AS IF THEY WERE SODOM AND GOMORRAH:
HAVE SOMEONE READ ISAIAH 1:10-17]**

10 Hear the word of the LORD, you rulers of Sodom; listen to the law of our God, you people of Gomorrah!

11 "The multitude of your sacrifices—what are they to me?" says the LORD. "I have more than enough of burnt offerings, of rams and the fat of fattened animals; I have no pleasure in the blood of bulls and lambs and goats.

12 When you come to appear before me, who has asked this of you, this trampling of my courts?

13 Stop bringing meaningless offerings! Your incense is detestable to me. New Moons, Sabbaths and convocations—I cannot bear your evil assemblies.

14 Your New Moon festivals and your appointed feasts my soul hates. They have become a burden to me; I am weary of bearing them.

15 When you spread out your hands in prayer, I will hide my eyes from you; even if you offer many prayers, I will not listen. Your hands are full of blood;

16 wash and make yourselves clean. Take your evil deeds out of my sight! Stop doing wrong,

17 learn to do right! Seek justice, encourage the oppressed. Defend the cause of the fatherless, plead the case of the widow."

? Am I the only one who feels uncomfortable reading this? What feelings does this passage raise for you?

? When push comes to shove, what does God seem to want more: worship or doing the right thing?

- Which do you think is easier: performing acts of worship or seeking justice? Because...

- Maybe this is obvious but, which do you see more of in the modern church: worship or seeking justice? Why do you think that is?

? Let's break out the list of actions God calls for in this passage. What does each of them mean to you?

- **verse 16:** "wash and make yourselves clean." What do you think that might look like for people like us in places like this?

- **verse 16:** "Take your evil deeds out of my sight!" What's that about...hiding better?

- **verse 16:** "Stop doing wrong." (Remember, Isaiah's audience isn't pagans, it's people who claim to follow God) What wrongdoing do you see today among people who claim to follow God?

- You don't have to answer out loud (unless you're brave or a little crazy) but, what wrongdoing have you seen in the mirror?

- **verse 17:** "Learn to do right!" If doing right were easy, everyone would do it. That's why it says "*learn* to do right." When it comes to justice, how do you think people learn to do right?

|||||
On a scale of one to five (one is not far along, five is nearly there), how far along do you think you are in learning to do right?

- **verse 17:** "Seek justice." Where does justice hide? Or is the question, "Who hides justice?"

- **verse 17:** "encourage the oppressed" (different translations render this different ways. For reasons you can probably guess, the NRSV is my favorite here; it says "rescue the oppressed.") Who are the oppressed in the world?

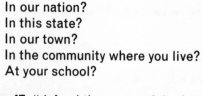

In our nation?
In this state?
In our town?
In the community where you live?
At your school?

- **verse 17:** "defend the cause of the fatherless." Who would you include among the fatherless?

- Why do you think they need defending?

- **verse 17:** "plead the case of the widow." Who takes advantage of the widows of the world?

- Why do widows need someone else to plead their case?

? If God's people don't do the things in these verses, who will?

OK; that's enough for now. Let's finish our time together with a little personal inventory.

[DISTRIBUTE THE SESSION ONE PERSONAL INVENTORY AND PENCILS]

ACTION

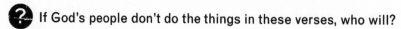

In the next four sessions, we'll try to understand and act on four big ideas.

First: God hates injustice. Hates it, hates it, hates it.

Second: One way or another, God calls every Christian to join the fight against injustice.

Third: God never, ever calls people to do something important, like fighting oppression, without providing everything it takes to do the job.

Fourth: There are specific, practical ways we can join the fight for justice. We'll get very specific about individual and group action.

Here are three things you can do this week:

||||||
WebSite: Visit IJM.com/Justice Mission for more about oppression, including a guide for praying about injustice.

||||||
Dig: Clip reports of bullying and oppression from newspapers, magazines and web sites and bring them to our next meeting.

||||||
Journal: At least every other day, journal about what you're seeing, hearing and feeling about oppression. **[handout]**

? To close our time together, may I ask three or four of you to read out loud the prayer you just wrote?

[IF NO ONE VOLUNTEERS, LET THEM OFF THE HOOK GENTLY AND CLOSE THE MEETING YOURSELF]

1. What do you think is the most important thing you've seen or heard or thought about in this session?

SESSION
1

2. Why do you think that's so important?

3. What do you think you'd like to do about your most important thing?

4. What questions do you want answered in the next session?

5. Write a prayer or poem or draw a picture to express your thoughts and feelings about justice and oppression in the world.

THE JUSTICE MISSION

Write about where you got YOUR IDEAS about oppression as a child.

Write about how your ideas on OPPRESSION have changed over time.

WE DON'T HAVE TO GO to India to find oppression—we don't even have to leave town.
Describe examples of oppression in our town or state.

A GREAT MANY beedie cigarettes are smoked by North Americans in their teens and 20s. Write about how that makes you feel since you saw the Oppression video.

IT COSTS the International Justice Mission an average of $500 US to gain freedom for a child trapped in bonded labor. Describe your thoughts and feelings about that.

THE JUSTICE MISSION

1

Write about how you think a BULLY turns into an oppressor.

Write about how you feel to be learning about injustice at THIS MOMENT in your life.

2

WHAT DOES GOD HATE?

THE JUSTICE MISSION 2
WHAT GOD HATES

STUFF

- **List-making** materials; Bibles or handouts; video playback; *The Justice Mission* video cued to *I Don't Get It*.

GATHERING

- **Brainstorm:** Oppressors Hall of Fame

VIDEO

- **Video-driven discussion:** I Don't Get It

OPERATING INSTRUCTIONS

- **Bible Study:** Job 24

THE BIG IDEA

- **Instruction:** Deception and Coercion (isolation, cover of authority, claim to legitimacy)

OPERATING INSTRUCTIONS

- **Bible Study:** Hebrews 13: 1-3

REFLECTION

- **Meditation:** Psalm 9

- **Personal Inventory:** What's most important?

ACTION

- **WordSearch:** Bible passages for personal reflection

- **Dig:** Community injustice inventory

- **Journal:** Personal Journaling

- **WebSite:** Find more at www.ijm.org/JusticeMission

THIS SESSION

A long time ago I worked on a video that featured Tony Campolo speaking to a group of adolescents about compassion. When I showed it to my youth group one boy said it was easy for Campolo to say that stuff about poor people, standing there in his five hundred dollar suit. "Scott," I said, "He dresses off the rack at JCPenney. That's the same fifty dollar corduroy jacket he always wears. What's your point?"

Scott's point was simple: he was angry because Tony was asking him to consider his responsibility to the poor. Scott didn't like being on the hook.

Who does? Life's complicated enough, right? Ignorance is bliss.

Life got more complicated for Ben, Charissa, Lindsay and Trever on their visit to India. They saw things they never expected to see—heard, smelled, saw and touched the inconceivable. To their credit, they all pushed through disbelief and skepticism to really see what was in front of them, really feel their feelings. That took courage.

Your group is half a world away from all that and, like my old friend Scott, some may feel irritated at being reminded that Christian faith embraces what God hates as much as what God loves. It's not comfortable for me; why would I expect it to be comfortable for a 15 year-old?

This session begins with a cognitive process (naming oppressors), then moves to an emotional exercise called *I Don't Get It*, a two-minute video designed to uncover hidden feelings in your group.[1]

Don't be shocked if some individuals seem less-than-positive about being asked to join the fight against injustice. Press on. If you connect with the skeptics, you'll really connect with the tenderhearted. And don't overlook the value a skeptic's questions can bring to your process: some kids take things to heart on a shallow and unconsidered level; the skeptic invites them to think deeper, which can lead to deeper conviction and long-lasting commitments. And wouldn't that be nice.

GATHERING

It's time for show and tell: If you saw an example of oppression this week, please tell us about it.

Let's make a list of famous oppressors and what they did that made them famous. I'll go first: **Joseph Stalin**.

 Anyone know what Stalin did? In the 1930s, Stalin ordered the murder of more than 600,000 Russian citizens and enforced policies that led to the starvation of six million Ukrainians.

---

[1] *I Don't Get It* is just two minutes long because that's how long it takes to reveal internal dialogues that could keep your group from pursuing the next step in fighting oppression—attitudes like, "It's too hard," or "It's not my job." Don't be surprised if this short clip generates as much discussion as the longer pieces. By the same token, there's a lot happening very fast in those two minutes, so don't hesitate to show it twice.

Let's list as many more oppressors as we can think of in the next few minutes.

[ASK SOMEONE TO MAKE THE LIST SO EVERYONE CAN SEE IT. IF YOUR GROUP DRAWS A BLANK, NAME SOME OF THE FOLLOWING OPPRESSORS AND SEE IF THEY CAN RECALL ANY DETAILS. NO NEED TO BELABOR THE POINT; STOP WHEN YOU THINK THEY'RE GETTING IT AND MOVE INTO THE QUESTIONS]

‖‖‖
Timothy McVeigh; convicted of killing 168 people in a terrorist bombing attack in Oklahoma City

‖‖‖
Pol Pot; Khmer Rouge leader; oversaw the extermination of at least a million people in Cambodia—perhaps twice that many.

‖‖‖
Adolph Hitler; Nazi leader; invaded nearly every country in Europe in a war that claimed thirty-three million lives—half of them civilians, six million of them European Jews detained, relocated and murdered in what may be history's most calculated ethnic cleansing.

‖‖‖
Jeffrey Dahmer; murdered, mutilated and ate 17 young men and boys in Milwaukee and Chicago.

‖‖‖
Idi Amin; dictator of Uganda; ordered the murder of an estimated 250,000 of his country's citizens.

‖‖‖
Augusto Pinochet; Chilean dictator; accused of causing the disappearance, torture and murder of at least 3,000 citizens.

‖‖‖
Ted Bundy; a charming, handsome man who raped, tortured and murdered 28 women and girls from Colorado to Florida.

‖‖‖
Slobodan Milosevic; Serbian leader; ordered the ethnic cleansing in Kosovo that killed a still-undetermined number of citizens and expelled over 700,000 from their homes.

‖‖‖
George Custer; poster boy for military operations that killed or relocated the entire population of native Americans following President Andrew Jackson's Indian Removal Act of 1830—though of course the process was underway long before that and continued long after.

‖‖‖
Former Rwandan Prime Minister **Jean Kambanda** and who-knows-how-many Hutu leaders whose genocide played out in the brutal murders of 800,000 Rwandan Tutsis in April and May of 1994.

‖‖‖
Governmental and medical personnel in Washington, DC, and Alabama who conducted the **Tuskegee Experiments** in which 399 African American men infected with syphilis were given bogus treatments for 40 years in order to observe the brutal progress of the fatal disease.
‖‖‖

Osama bin Laden; architect of the murders of dozens of sailors aboard the U.S.S. Cole, hundreds in U.S. Embassy bombings in Africa and thousands in attacks on the World Trade Center and Pentagon.

Describe the range of emotions you felt as we went through the list of oppressors.

[IF YOU WANT TO CREATE PHYSICAL MOVEMENT IN YOUR GROUP, HAVE PEOPLE MOVE TO PLACES IN THE ROOM THAT CORRESPOND WITH THEIR FEELINGS OF NUMBNESS, HELPLESSNESS, FURY, OR DETERMINATION TO CHANGE THINGS]

- Who felt helpless? Talk about that.
- Who felt angry? How angry are you? What do you feel like doing?
- Who felt determined to change things? What do you want to do?
- Who felt numb? Talk about that.
- What did I leave out? Talk about that?

VIDEO: I DON'T GET IT.

 I want to show you a video clip. Watch carefully because it happens very fast. It's called **I Don't Get It.**

I DON'T GET IT

injustice

oppression

abuse of power

it's **none** of **my business**

I don't know those people
they're not bothering me

even if they were...
I'm just a kid.
cut me some slack here

sex slaves
widows
orphans
bonded labor
cops killing street kids
kidnapping
forced relocation

what am I supposed to do about that?

you want me to feel bad?
fine. **I feel bad.**
now what?

it's halfway around the world and I'm just a kid

If it's so important
why haven't our parents
fixed it already

I don't get it
I mean, really
isn't that what God is
supposed to do?

I'm **sympathetic** and **all**
but really?
I don't see how that stuff
is any of my business

even if it were...
I'm just a kid
(I guess I said that
already)

look
I don't wanna feel bad
I want to feel useful
gimme something I can do

just help me **understand**
if there's something to be
done
I'll do it

if I thought I could
actually make a difference
if I really believed
God had a plan
— and it was me —
nothing could **stop me**

2

THE JUSTICE MISSION

[WHEN THE VIDEO ENDS, PASS OUT THE HANDOUT TEXT (PHOTOCOPIED OR DOWN-LOADED); OR READ POEM, AND ASK:]

? What image or line stands out for you in that clip? Why do you think that's significant?

? What statement or question most nearly expresses your thoughts and feelings today?

? What do you think of the argument, "I'm just a kid"?

? What's your reaction to the line, "If it's so important why haven't our parents fixed it already?"

? What's your reaction to the line, "Isn't that what God is supposed to do?"

? What's your reaction to the lines, "I don't want to feel bad, I want to feel useful. If I really believed God had a plan—and it was me— nothing could stop me"?

- Is that true for you? How would feel if you found out you could do something to bring justice to oppressed people?

> Before we go on, let's stop a moment and ask God to help us understand his feelings and attitudes about oppression.

[HAVE SOMEONE PRAY, OR PRAY YOURSELF, OR LEAVE A FEW MOMENTS OF SILENCE, BEFORE YOU CONTINUE.]

OPERATING INSTRUCTIONS

> Let's read Job 24 together and talk about it.

[BY THE TIME WE GET TO CHAPTER 24, JOB HAS LOST JUST ABOUT EVERYTHING THAT MATTERS TO HIM — HIS FAMILY IS GONE, HIS HOME IS DESTROYED, HIS HEALTH IS RUINED, HIS REPUTATION IS DAMAGED BEYOND REPAIR. AND JOB'S THREE "COMFORTERS" HAVE JUST ABOUT COMFORTED HIM TO DEATH WITH NAGGING QUESTIONS AND SELF-RIGHTEOUS LECTURES ABOUT THE WAYS OF GOD. NOW JOB FILES A COMPLAINT AGAINST GOD, WONDERING WHY THE ALMIGHTY SEEMS TO BE AN UNDERACHIEVER IN THE FIGHT AGAINST OPPRESSION.]

[READ VERSE ONE OF JOB 24]

1 "Why does the Almighty not set times for judgment? Why must those who know him look in vain for such days?

? Have you ever heard this question?

- Raise your hand if you ever asked this question yourself.

- What do you think is the answer?

As we read on, see how many varieties of oppression you hear. In fact, whenever you hear an injustice, say, "Well that ain't right." Let's practice: three, two, one, "Well that ain't right."

[IF YOU DOUBT YOUR GROUP WILL GO ALONG WITH THIS GAG, A SIMPLE RAISING OF HANDS WILL DO. OR HAVE THEM STAND UP WHEN THEY HEAR AN INJUSTICE, THEN SIT DOWN WHEN THEY HEAR THE NEXT ONE, AND SO ON. HAVE SOME FUN WITH IT IF YOU CAN.]

IIIII
OK, here we go:

2 Men move boundary stones; **[PAUSE TO LEAD THE GROUP IN SAYING, "WELL THAT AIN'T RIGHT!" THEN ADD THAT ONE WAY OPPRESSORS STEAL LAND IS SIMPLY BY MOVING THE BOUNDARY MARKERS ON A POOR FARMER'S PROPERTY, THEN DARING HIM TO PROVE THEY DID IT. THEN PICK UP WITH THE NEXT VERSE.]**

2 they pasture flocks they have stolen. **["WELL THAT AIN'T RIGHT!"]**

3 They drive away the orphan's donkey and take the widow's ox in pledge. **["WELL THAT AIN'T RIGHT!"]**

4 They thrust the needy from the path and force all the poor of the land into hiding. **["WELL THAT AIN'T RIGHT!"]**

OK, there's a lot of stuff here that just ain't right. For example, "taking the widow's ox in pledge "means holding it as the guarantee on a loan until she gets the plowing done"—which she can't do without the ox.

IIIII
Let me keep reading:

5 Like wild donkeys in the desert, the poor go about their labor of foraging food; the wasteland provides food for their children.

6 They gather fodder in the fields and glean in the vineyards of the wicked.

7 Lacking clothes, they spend the night naked; they have nothing to cover themselves in the cold.

8 They are drenched by mountain rains and hug the rocks for lack of shelter.

9 The fatherless child is snatched from the breast; the infant of the poor is seized for a debt.

10 Lacking clothes, they go about naked; they carry the sheaves, but still go hungry.

11 They crush olives among the terraces; they tread the winepresses, yet suffer thirst.

12 The groans of the dying rise from the city, and the souls of the wounded cry out for help. But God charges no one with wrongdoing.

13 There are those who rebel against the light, who do not know its ways or stay in its paths.

14 When daylight is gone, the murderer rises up and kills the poor and needy; in the night he steals forth like a thief.

15 The eye of the adulterer watches for dusk; he thinks, 'No eye will see me,' and he keeps his face concealed.

THE JUSTICE MISSION

16 In the dark, men break into houses, but by day they shut themselves in; they want nothing to do with the light.

17 For all of them, deep darkness is their morning; they make friends with the terrors of darkness."

> You know what? That sure ain't right. The poor and the weak don't have a chance against people like that.

 What are some ways people respond when they're the victims of oppression?

[AS PEOPLE IDENTIFY A WAY VICTIMS RESPOND — DESPAIR, FOR EXAMPLE, OR VIOLENCE, OR GIVING UP — ASK:]

- Do you think that's an appropriate response? Because...

THE BIG IDEA

> Oppressors attack their victims with two weapons: **Coercion** and **Deception**.

‖‖‖‖
Coercion is force. Coercion is ganging up, physical intimidation, rape, terrorism, invasion

‖‖‖‖
Deception is lying in all its forms. For example:

- **withholding** information

- **suppressing** information (prohibiting truthful reports in the press)

- **misinformation** (misleading people)

- **disinformation** (outright lies)

- **propaganda** (making one side of a story look better than it is and the other side look worse).

[YOU MAY WANT TO STOP HERE—COERCION AND DECEPTION MAY BE AS MUCH AS YOUR GROUP CAN GET THEIR ARMS AROUND AT THIS POINT (IF SO, SKIP TO JOB 24:18). IF YOU WANT MORE INFORMATION, YOU CAN EXPLAIN THE WEAPONS OPPRESSORS USE, A BIT FURTHER BELOW.]

We can break the weapons of oppressors down further. The three primary ways oppressors use force and lies are *isolation*, the *cover of authority* and the *claim to legitimacy*.

‖‖‖‖
Isolation is building a wall around law-abiding citizens to hide the exact nature and extent of injustice. Isolation includes unjust imprisonment; "disappearing" people through kidnapping or murder; partitioning communities so they lose contact with the outside world; displacing people so they lose their network of family, friends and associates; dispersing groups so they can no longer cooperate and support each other; relocating individuals or

groups against their will; unjust legal and economic practices (like racial profiling and redlining) that keep people from making a living or finding a place to live.

> **Profiling** is singling out a religious, racial or ethnic minority for unjust treatment by law enforcement. **Redlining** is a form of profiling in which, for example, banks are discouraged from lending money so people of a minority population can purchase homes in a particular neighborhood.

The **cover of authority** shields oppressors from the consequences of abuse against law-abiding people by police, military and legislatures.

The **claim to legitimacy** says: "We're the good guys no matter what we do" and seems to crop up around military coups, rebellions, terrorism, and invasions.

Oppressors use some or all these weapons against their victims. Can you think of any real life examples of *isolation,* the *cover of authority* or the *claim to legitimacy* as weapons of oppression?

Let's finish our reading at Job 24:18. Here's what's in store for oppressors:

18 "Yet they are foam on the surface of the water; their portion of the land is cursed, so that no one goes to the vineyards.

19 As heat and drought snatch away the melted snow, so the grave snatches away those who have sinned.

20 The womb forgets them, the worm feasts on them; evil men are no longer remembered but are broken like a tree.

21 They prey on the barren and childless woman, and to the widow show no kindness.

22 But God drags away the mighty by his power; though they become established, they have no assurance of life.

23 He may let them rest in a feeling of security, but his eyes are on their ways.

24 For a little while they are exalted, and then they are gone; they are brought low and gathered up like all others; they are cut off like heads of grain.

25 "If this is not so, who can prove me false and reduce my words to nothing?"

> Job throws down a challenge in verse 25. In essence, he says: "Sooner or later, oppressors live to regret their injustice. If you doubt that, show me an exception."

 Do you think Job is right? What evidence do you have to support your thoughts about this?

[IF YOU HAVE TIME, COMPARE JOB'S THOUGHTS WITH PSALM 73]

THE JUSTICE MISSION

Psalm 73

A Psalm of Asaph.

1 Surely God is good to Israel, to those who are pure in heart.

2 But as for me, my feet had almost slipped; I had nearly lost my foothold.

3 For I envied the arrogant when I saw the prosperity of the wicked.

4 They have no struggles; their bodies are healthy and strong.

5 They are free from the burdens common to man; they are not plagued by human ills.

6 Therefore pride is their necklace; they clothe themselves with violence.

7 From their callous hearts comes iniquity; the evil conceits of their minds know no limits.

8 They scoff, and speak with malice; in their arrogance they threaten oppression.

9 Their mouths lay claim to heaven, and their tongues take possession of the earth.

10 Therefore their people turn to them and drink up waters in abundance.

11 They say, "How can God know? Does the Most High have knowledge?"

12 This is what the wicked are like—always carefree, they increase in wealth.

13 Surely in vain have I kept my heart pure; in vain have I washed my hands in innocence.

14 All day long I have been plagued; I have been punished every morning.

15 If I had said, "I will speak thus," I would have betrayed your children.

16 When I tried to understand all this, it was oppressive to me

17 till I entered the sanctuary of God; then I understood their final destiny.

18 Surely you place them on slippery ground; you cast them down to ruin.

19 How suddenly are they destroyed, completely swept away by terrors!

20 As a dream when one awakes, so when you arise, O Lord, you will despise them as fantasies.

21 When my heart was grieved and my spirit embittered,

22 I was senseless and ignorant; I was a brute beast before you.

23 Yet I am always with you; you hold me by my right hand.

24 You guide me with your counsel, and afterward you will take me into glory.

25 Whom have I in heaven but you? And earth has nothing I desire besides you.

26 My flesh and my heart may fail, but God is the strength of my heart and my portion forever.

27 Those who are far from you will perish; you destroy all who are unfaithful to you.

28 But as for me, it is good to be near God. I have made the Sovereign LORD my refuge; I will tell of all your deeds.

OPERATING INSTRUCTIONS

Look at Hebrews 13:1-3

1 Keep on loving each other as brothers.

2 Do not forget to entertain strangers, for by so doing some people have entertained angels without knowing it.

3 Remember those in prison as if you were their fellow prisoners, and those who are mistreated as if you yourselves were suffering.

> Let's list the human beings in these three verses.

[WRITE DOWN THE LIST, INCLUDING BROTHERS (AND SISTERS), STRANGERS, PRISONERS, VICTIMS, US—BY THE WAY, IN THE BIBLE, "STRANGER" USUALLY REFERS TO A RESIDENT ALIEN.]

How does the passage describe our responsibility to each of these?

What's your biggest challenge in loving other Christians as if they were your brothers and sisters?

What's your biggest challenge in being hospitable to aliens and strangers?

What's the biggest challenge to remembering prisoners as if you were in jail too?

What's your biggest challenge in remembering those who are mistreated as if you were suffering yourself?

What's the biggest challenge to actually *doing* something about oppression?

- What do you think it will take to overcome that?

REFLECTION

What do you think is the most important thing you've seen or heard or thought about in this session?

Why do you think that's so important compared with the rest?

What do you think you'd like to do about your most important thing?

What questions do you want answers for in the next session?

Write a prayer or poem or draw a picture to express your thoughts and feelings about justice and injustice in the world.

ACTION

Here are four things you can do before we get together again.

▐▐▐▐
WordSearch: Spend five or 10 minutes with one of these passages several days this week; ask God to help you understand what you're reading and I promise you'll know more about God and more about yourself the next time we're together. Fair enough? **[handout]**

▐▐▐▐
Dig: Ask about, read about, find out about past and present injustice in our community. What does it cost to fight injustice in our community (think law enforcement, care for victims of domestic violence, sexual assault crisis centers, that kind of thing). Plan to tell us what you dig up next week.

THE JUSTICE MISSION

|||||
Journal: At least every other day this week, journal about what you're seeing, hearing and feeling about oppression. **[handout]**

|||||
WebSite: Go to www.IJM.org/JusticeMission for more about loving what God loves and hating what God hates.

? Who wants to pray for us now as we finish up?

HERE'S THE PROMISE:

- If you spend five or ten minutes with one or more of these passages several times this week...

- If you ask God to help you understand what you're reading...

- If you're open to loving what God loves and hating what God hates...

...by this time next week you'll know more about God and more about yourself. **That's a promise.**

Proverbs 14:31

He who oppresses the poor shows contempt for their Maker, but whoever is kind to the needy honors God.

Psalm 146

1 Praise the LORD. Praise the LORD, O my soul.

2 I will praise the LORD all my life; I will sing praise to my God as long as I live.

3 Do not put your trust in princes, in mortal men, who cannot save.

4 When their spirit departs, they return to the ground; on that very day their plans come to nothing.

5 Blessed is he whose help is the God of Jacob, whose hope is in the LORD his God,

6 the Maker of heaven and earth, the sea, and everything in them—the LORD, who remains faithful forever.

7 He upholds the cause of the oppressed and gives food to the hungry. The LORD sets prisoners free,

8 the LORD gives sight to the blind, the LORD lifts up those who are bowed down, the LORD loves the righteous.

9 The LORD watches over the alien and sustains the fatherless and the widow, but he frustrates the ways of the wicked.

10 The LORD reigns forever, your God, O Zion, for all generations. Praise the LORD.

Psalm 10

1 Why, O LORD, do you stand far off? Why do you hide yourself in times of trouble?

2 In his arrogance the wicked man hunts down the weak, who are caught in the schemes he devises.

3 He boasts of the cravings of his heart; he blesses the greedy and reviles the LORD.

4 In his pride the wicked does not seek him; in all his thoughts there is no room for God.

5 His ways are always prosperous; he is haughty and your laws are far from him; he sneers at all his enemies.

6 He says to himself, "Nothing will shake me; I'll always be happy and never have trouble."

7 His mouth is full of curses and lies and threats; trouble and evil are under his tongue.

8 He lies in wait near the villages; from ambush he murders the innocent, watching in secret for his victims.

9 He lies in wait like a lion in cover; he lies in wait to catch the helpless; he catches the helpless and drags them off in his net.

10 His victims are crushed, they collapse; they fall under his strength.

11 He says to himself, "God has forgotten; he covers his face and never sees."

12 Arise, LORD! Lift up your hand, O God. Do not forget the helpless.

13 Why does the wicked man revile God? Why does he say to himself, "He won't call me to account"?

14 But you, O God, do see trouble and grief; you consider it to take it in hand. The victim commits himself to you; you are the helper of the fatherless.

15 Break the arm of the wicked and evil man; call him to account for his wickedness that would not be found out.

16 The LORD is King for ever and ever; the nations will perish from his land.

17 You hear, O LORD, the desire of the afflicted; you encourage them, and you listen to their cry,

18 defending the fatherless and the oppressed, in order that man, who is of the earth, may terrify no more.

Matthew 12:9-21

9 Going on from that place, he went into their synagogue,

10 and a man with a shriveled hand was there. Looking for a reason to accuse Jesus, they asked him, "Is it lawful to heal on the Sabbath?"

11 He said to them, "If any of you has a sheep and it falls into a pit on the Sabbath, will you not take hold of it and lift it out?

12 How much more valuable is a man than a sheep! Therefore it is lawful to do good on the Sabbath."

13 Then he said to the man, "Stretch out your hand." So he stretched it out and it was completely restored, just as sound as the other.

14 But the Pharisees went out and plotted how they might kill Jesus.

15 Aware of this, Jesus withdrew from that place. Many followed him, and he healed all their sick,

THE JUSTICE MISSION

16 warning them not to tell who he was.

17 This was to fulfill what was spoken through the prophet Isaiah:

18 "Here is my servant whom I have chosen, the one I love, in whom I delight; I will put my Spirit on him, and he will proclaim justice to the nations.

19 He will not quarrel or cry out; no one will hear his voice in the streets.

20 A bruised reed he will not break, and a smoldering wick he will not snuff out, till he leads justice to victory.

21 In his name the nations will put their hope."

Psalm 73

A psalm of Asaph.

1 Surely God is good to Israel, to those who are pure in heart.

2 But as for me, my feet had almost slipped; I had nearly lost my foothold.

3 For I envied the arrogant when I saw the prosperity of the wicked.

4 They have no struggles; their bodies are healthy and strong.

5 They are free from the burdens common to man; they are not plagued by human ills.

6 Therefore pride is their necklace; they clothe themselves with violence.

7 From their callous hearts comes iniquity; the evil conceits of their minds know no limits.

8 They scoff, and speak with malice; in their arrogance they threaten oppression.

9 Their mouths lay claim to heaven, and their tongues take possession of the earth.

10 Therefore their people turn to them and drink up waters in abundance.

11 They say, "How can God know? Does the Most High have knowledge?"

12 This is what the wicked are like—always carefree, they increase in wealth.

13 Surely in vain have I kept my heart pure; in vain have I washed my hands in innocence.

14 All day long I have been plagued; I have been punished every morning.

15 If I had said, "I will speak thus," I would have betrayed your children.

16 When I tried to understand all this, it was oppressive to me

17 till I entered the sanctuary of God; then I understood their final destiny.

18 Surely you place them on slippery ground; you cast them down to ruin.

19 How suddenly are they destroyed, completely swept away by terrors!

20 As a dream when one awakes, so when you arise, O Lord, you will despise them as fantasies.

21 When my heart was grieved and my spirit embittered,

22 I was senseless and ignorant; I was a brute beast before you.

23 Yet I am always with you; you hold me by my right hand.

24 You guide me with your counsel, and afterward you will take me into glory.

25 Whom have I in heaven but you? And earth has nothing I desire besides you.

26 My flesh and my heart may fail, but God is the strength of my heart and my portion forever.

27 Those who are far from you will perish; you destroy all who are unfaithful to you.

28 But as for me, it is good to be near God. I have made the Sovereign LORD my refuge; I will tell of all your deeds.

Psalm 9

1 I will praise you, O LORD, with all my heart; I will tell of all your wonders.

2 I will be glad and rejoice in you; I will sing praise to your name, O Most High.

3 My enemies turn back; they stumble and perish before you.

4 For you have upheld my right and my cause; you have sat on your throne, judging righteously.

5 You have rebuked the nations and destroyed the wicked; you have blotted out their name for ever and ever.

6 Endless ruin has overtaken the enemy, you have uprooted their cities; even the memory of them has perished.

7 The LORD reigns forever; he has established his throne for judgment.

8 He will judge the world in righteousness; he will govern the peoples with justice.

9 The LORD is a refuge for the oppressed, a stronghold in times of trouble.

10 Those who know your name will trust in you, for you, LORD, have never forsaken those who seek you.

11 Sing praises to the LORD, enthroned in Zion; proclaim among the nations what he has done.

12 For he who avenges blood remembers; he does not ignore the cry of the afflicted.

13 O LORD, see how my enemies persecute me! Have mercy and lift me up from the gates of death,

14 that I may declare your praises in the gates of the Daughter of Zion and there rejoice in your salvation.

15 The nations have fallen into the pit they have dug; their feet are caught in the net they have hidden.

16 The LORD is known by his justice; the wicked are ensnared by the work of their hands.

17 The wicked return to the grave, all the nations that forget God.

18 But the needy will not always be forgotten, nor the hope of the afflicted ever perish.

19 Arise, O LORD, let not man triumph; let the nations be judged in your presence.

20 Strike them with terror, O LORD; let the nations know they are but men.

THE JUSTICE MISSION

1. What do you think is the most important thing you've seen or heard or thought about in this session?

2. Why do you think that's so important compared with the rest?

SESSION

2

THE JUSTICE MISSION

3. What do you think you'd like to do about your most important thing?

4. What questions do you want answers for in the next session?

5. Write a prayer or poem or draw a picture to express your thoughts and feelings about justice and injustice in the world.

It costs the International Justice Mission an average of $1000 US to gain freedom for a girl
trapped in FORCED PROSTITUTION. Describe your
thoughts and feelings about that.

Write about your feelings toward the victims of injustice in OUR TOWN or STATE.
Compare those feelings to your emotional response to victims of injustice in poor
societies like India.

2

Write about the way you think GOD SEES
oppressors.

Write about what you think your PARENTS' GENERATION has done to fight oppression.

Write about God's responsibility to do justice for the oppressed.

THE JUSTICE MISSION

2

Write about the OBSTACLES to doing justice in your generation.

Write as SPECIFICALLY as you can about how you think you want to respond to injustice.

3

THE JUSTICE MISSION 3
JOINING THE FIGHT AGAINST INJUSTICE.

STUFF

● A baby, five or six months of age (no kidding: if the child is too old, the gag won't work); Bibles; list-making materials; response lists; video playback and *The Justice Mission* video cued to *Remembering Justice.*

GATHERING

● **Object Lesson and Discussion:** Object Permanence

OPERATING INSTRUCTIONS

● **Bible Study:** Isaiah 58

THE BIG IDEA

● **Video-driven Discussion:** Remembering Justice

REFLECTION

● **Meditation:** Psalm 146

● **Personal Inventory:** What can I do?

ACTION

● **Website:** IJM web site

● **Dig:** targeted media search

● **Dig:** Interview someone who fights injustice

● **Journal:** Personal Journaling

THIS SESSION

In Apostolic times, justice followed Christians wherever they went because followers of Jesus loved justice and worked for justice.

After the Apostle Paul presented his understanding of the Gospel to the Church leaders in Jerusalem, the only thing they asked was that he continue to remember the poor (which he was already eager to do). Christians in Rome took it on themselves to rescue newborns routinely abandoned in the city dumps, and it was Christians who finally succeeded in putting an end to the gladiatorial games.

And so it went for most of 20 centuries—Christians taking up the cause of the weak and oppressed as a natural expression of the life of Christ in them—even when seeking justice was difficult.

But, it must be said, in some times and places, Christians forgot the call to do justice, love mercy, and walk humbly with God (Think the (un)Holy Crusades, think the Spanish Inquisition, think Columbus and the genocide of the native population of Hispañola—add your own list of church-supported atrocities here.)

In the last half of the 20th century, some Christians have been too preoccupied with self-definition and self-preservation to maintain a sharp edge on creating justice in Jesus' name. Whatever the reason (you could spend a week reading various accounts and explanations), with rare exceptions, we seem simply to have forgotten how to do justice. How it happened, and why, is a conversation for another day. Today, the subject is *remembering*.

Today we meet some Christians who are recapturing God's mandate to pursue justice: the International Justice Mission.

The International Justice Mission is a group of attorneys, diplomats and law enforcement officers who love Jesus and are committed to establishing justice in his name for the oppressed.

In this session, Ben, Charissa, Lindsay and Trever are eyewitnesses to how IJM practices the ancient art of doing justice in a new century.

And, just to be clear: This is not a commercial for IJM, it's an endorsement of the sort we reserve for special occasions. The folks at IJM deliver the real deal. May their tribe increase.

GATHERING

Did you find out anything about the history of oppression in our community this week? **[If yes, ask for details]**

- Any other insights into oppression and justice this week?

What's the most embarrassing thing you ever forgot? **[IF YOU DON'T HAVE ANY OF YOUR OWN, BORROW ONE OF MINE: I FORGOT TO CHECK MY MOM'S FLIGHT SCHEDULE AND LEFT HER AND MY STEP-FATHER STRANDED AT THE AIRPORT FOR THREE HOURS; I FORGOT TO CHECK MY FIGURES AND DIDN'T SEND MY DAUGHTER ENOUGH MONEY FOR HER LAST SEMESTER IN COLLEGE...YIKES!]**

3

THE JUSTICE MISSION

[ASK PEOPLE TO LOOK UP THE FOLLOWING BIBLE PASSAGES AND READ THEM ALOUD TO THE GROUP OR SET IT UP AS A BRIEF READERS THEATER PERFORMANCE]

Deuteronomy 32:18 You deserted the Rock, who fathered you; you forgot the God who gave you birth.

Isaiah 17:10 You have forgotten God your Savior; you have not remembered the Rock, your fortress. Therefore, though you set out the finest plants and plant imported vines,

Jeremiah 2:32 Does a maiden forget her jewelry, a bride her wedding ornaments? Yet my people have forgotten me, days without number.

Jeremiah 3:21 A cry is heard on the barren heights, the weeping and pleading of the people of Israel, because they have perverted their ways and have forgotten the LORD their God.

Jeremiah 13:25 This is your lot, the portion I have decreed for you," declares the LORD, "because you have forgotten me and trusted in false gods.

Jeremiah 18:15 Yet my people have forgotten me; they burn incense to worthless idols, which made them stumble in their ways and in the ancient paths. They made them walk in bypaths and on roads not built up.

Ezekiel 22:12 In you men accept bribes to shed blood; you take usury and excessive interest and make unjust gain from your neighbors by extortion. And you have forgotten me, declares the Sovereign LORD.

Again, a little something from my list of forgetfulness: for about 20 years, I forgot grace and acted like I had to (and actually could) earn God's approval; I forgot how much God loves me, so I lived in fear for years and years. **How about you?** Have you forgotten anything important?

❓ Why do you think people forget God?

- Do you think it has anything to do with the times when God seems to go silent for a while?

❓ What happens to God's love when it's out of sight?

- Are you sure? What makes you think that?

[BORROW A BABY AND PLAY PEEKABOO WITH A TOY (ANYONE OVER ABOUT FOUR MONTHS IS A RISKY CHOICE AS SHE MAY ALREADY BE IN ON THE GAME). ASK, "WHERE DID IT GO?" AS THE CHILD ENJOYS THE GAME. IF NO ONE WILL TRUST YOU WITH A CHILD, DESCRIBE THE PEEKABOO GAME. NEXT, PLAY PEEKABOO WITH AN ADOLESCENT VOLUNTEER. ASK, "WHERE DID IT GO?" UNTIL HE OR SHE DELIVERS THE PUNCH LINE: "IT'S BEHIND YOUR BACK, MORON," OR WHATEVER.]

❓ How do you know the toy didn't disappear?

> That phenomenon is called "object permanence." Past a certain point, people know objects don't cease to exist when they disappear from view. That's true of toys; it's true of God's love. It's also true of oppression and suffering.

Shortly after the 1985 Live Aid concert that raised $200 million for food relief in Africa [Bono and his wife Ali] *visited Ethiopia. They saw how quickly even $200 million in aid was depleted.*[1]

"We promised that we would never forget what we had been through," he said in a recent speech. "But of course we did."[2]

? Have you ever experienced the kind of forgetfulness Bono talked about—forgetting about good intentions?

- Why do you think that happens?

- In general, do you think this kind of forgetfulness leads to good outcomes or not so good? Why is that?

Edmund Burke (who lived in 18th century England) said, "The only thing necessary for the triumph of evil is for good men to do nothing."

? What do you think about that?

- Can you think of specific examples of evil winning because good folk failed to act? Talk about that.

Oppressors depend on the silence of people who could make a difference if they spoke up. Listen to this confession from a German pastor, Martin Niemoller, in the 1940's.

"In Germany they came first for the Communists and I didn't speak up because I wasn't a Communist. Then they came for the Jews and I didn't speak up because I wasn't a Jew. Then they came for the trade unionists and I didn't speak up because I wasn't a trade unionist. Then they came for the Catholics and I didn't speak up because I was a Protestant. Then they came for me—and by that time no one was left to speak up."

? What do you think about Pastor Niemoller's confession?

? Have you ever seen oppression—small or large—but failed to speak up for the oppressed?

- How do you feel about that today?

OPERATING INSTRUCTIONS

[ON THE SURFACE, FASTING INVOLVES GIVING UP FOOD FOR A WHILE. PLEASE DON'T LET IT GO AT THAT. THIS PASSAGE IS ABOUT WHAT'S BEHIND AND BENEATH AND INSIDE FASTING. WHAT GOD TELLS ISAIAH IS MORE ABOUT DOING JUSTICE THAN SKIPPING MEALS.]

---

[1] U2 singer, Bono, in *USA Today*, 06.15.01, p.2
[2] *Details*, November, 2001, talking about the need for debt relief for the world's poorest nations

THE JUSTICE MISSION

Let's look at Isaiah 58:1-5

1 "Shout it aloud, do not hold back. Raise your voice like a trumpet. Declare to my people their rebellion and to the house of Jacob their sins.

2 For day after day they seek me out; they seem eager to know my ways, as if they were a nation that does what is right and has not forsaken the commands of its God. They ask me for just decisions and seem eager for God to come near them.

3 'Why have we fasted,' they say, 'and you have not seen it? Why have we humbled ourselves, and you have not noticed?' "Yet on the day of your fasting, you do as you please and exploit all your workers.

4 Your fasting ends in quarreling and strife, and in striking each other with wicked fists. You cannot fast as you do today and expect your voice to be heard on high.

5 Is this the kind of fast I have chosen, only a day for a man to humble himself? Is it only for bowing one's head like a reed and for lying on sackcloth and ashes? Is that what you call a fast, a day acceptable to the LORD?"

What do you know about fasting?

["FASTING" MEANS "TO COVER OVER THE MOUTH" (STRONG'S CONCORDANCE). THE PRACTICE OF RESTRICTING FOOD WAS COMMON AMONG ANCIENT PEOPLE AS AN EXPRESSION OF DEVOTION TO GOD.]

What's wrong with the fasting described in the verses we just read?

- Do you think it's possible God might say the same thing about worship music or going to church or other expressions of devotion? Talk about that.

The next two verses describe the kind of devotion God appreciates.

Isaiah 58:6-7

6 "Is not this the kind of fasting I have chosen: to loose the chains of injustice and untie the cords of the yoke, to set the oppressed free and break every yoke?

7 Is it not to share your food with the hungry and to provide the poor wanderer with shelter—when you see the naked, to clothe him, and not to turn away from your own flesh and blood?

How does God's idea of fasting compare with what we read before?

- Can you name some "chains of injustice" you think need to be loosed today?
- ...any oppressed people you think need to be freed?
- ...any yokes you think need to be broken?

[FARMERS AND TEAMSTERS USE YOKES TO KEEP A BEAST OF BURDEN ATTACHED TO HIS LABOR]

- Can you think of practical ways to share your food with the hungry?

- ...ways to provide shelter to poor wanderers?

- ... ways to notice the naked and clothe them?

- ...ways you can turn toward your own flesh and blood instead of away from them?

> Pick up at verse eight to see what God promises when people fast his way.

Isaiah 58:8-14

8 Then your light will break forth like the dawn, and your healing will quickly appear; then your righteousness will go before you, and the glory of the LORD will be your rear guard.

9 Then you will call, and the LORD will answer; you will cry for help, and he will say: Here am I. "If you do away with the yoke of oppression, with the pointing finger and malicious talk,

10 and if you spend yourselves in behalf of the hungry and satisfy the needs of the oppressed, then your light will rise in the darkness, and your night will become like the noonday.

11 The LORD will guide you always; he will satisfy your needs in a sun-scorched land and will strengthen your frame. You will be like a well-watered garden, like a spring whose waters never fail.

12 Your people will rebuild the ancient ruins and will raise up the age-old foundations; you will be called Repairer of Broken Walls, Restorer of Streets with Dwellings.

13 "If you keep your feet from breaking the Sabbath and from doing as you please on my holy day, if you call the Sabbath a delight and the LORD'S holy day honorable, and if you honor it by not going your own way and not doing as you please or speaking idle words,

14 then you will find your joy in the LORD, and I will cause you to ride on the heights of the land and to feast on the inheritance of your father Jacob." The mouth of the LORD has spoken.

What do you think it means when God asks worshippers to do away with the yoke of oppression? **[VERSE 9]**

- What do you think that might look like in instances of forced labor or sexual slavery?

How would your day to day life be different if you spent yourself on behalf of the hungry and satisfied the needs of the oppressed? **[VERSE 10]**

- Is there anything that makes it difficult for you to live like that? Talk about that.

VIDEO: REMEMBERING JUSTICE

I want to show you a short video. It's called *Remembering Justice.*

[AS THE VIDEO ENDS, ASK:]

3

THE JUSTICE MISSION

? What story or image or idea stands out for you from the video?

● Why do you think that's significant?

? Back in the day, Christians were known for fighting injustice. What do you think Christians are known for today?

● How do you feel about that?

> Bob says what Ben, Charissa, Lindsay and Trever experienced is just the tip of the iceberg, meaning there's lots more oppression going on in lots more places around the world.

? Are you more energized or paralyzed by that thought?

▌▌▌▌ Stand up **[OR RAISE YOUR HAND OR LIFT YOUR RIGHT SHOE IN THE AIR]** if you're more energized by the scope of this problem.

● Tell us why you find that energizing.

▌▌▌▌ Stand up **[OR RAISE YOUR HAND OR LIFT YOUR RIGHT SHOE IN THE AIR]** if you're more paralyzed by the scope of this problem.

● Tell us why you find that paralyzing.

> **Proverbs 14:31** He who oppresses the poor shows contempt for their Maker, but whoever is kind to the needy honors God.
> **Micah 6:8** He has showed you, O man, what is good. And what does the LORD require of you? To act justly and to love mercy and to walk humbly with your God.
> **Matthew 23:23** "Woe to you, teachers of the law and Pharisees, you hypocrites! You give a tenth of your spices—mint, dill and cumin. But you have neglected the more important matters of the law—justice, mercy and faithfulness. You should have practiced the latter, without neglecting the former."

? Gary says loving a person in bonded labor or forced prostitution means doing what is necessary to bring them out. What do you think about that?

▌▌▌▌ Based on what we saw in the video, how effective do you think the International Justice Mission is in bringing people out of oppression?

● What did you see or hear that gave you that impression?

? Ben talked about the way IJM fights deception and coercion with truth and legal authority.

‖‖‖
On a scale of one to five (one is easy, five is difficult) how hard did that process seem to you? Talk about that.

? Charissa was surprised to learn it's no good just paying off the debt. Did you understand the reason for that?

[PAYING OFF THE DEBT IS A GOOD-HEARTED BUT SOFT-HEADED ATTEMPT TO SOLVE THE PROBLEM. THE MONEY-LENDERS ARE CRIMINALS, NOT BUSINESSMEN; THEY'RE HAPPY TO TAKE THE MONEY FROM WELL-MEANING OUTSIDERS AND THEN FIND A WAY TO TRICK OR FORCE THEIR VICTIMS BACK INTO THE SAME SITUATION SO THEY CAN DO IT ALL AGAIN. BY CONTRAST, IT COSTS IJM AN AVERAGE OF $500 TO FIND A LEGAL REMEDY FOR A PERSON IN BONDED LABOR, ABOUT $1000 FOR A PERSON IN FORCED PROSTITUTION, WHICH IS A WHOLE LOT MORE THAN THE ORIGINAL LOAN, BUT NOT ALL THAT COSTLY FOR A PERMANENT SOLUTION TO THE PROBLEM]

> It costs IJM an average of $500 to find a legal remedy for a person in bonded labor, about $1000 for a person in forced prostitution.

? Do those numbers strike you as low, high or what you would expect to pay for a permanent solution to one person's oppression?

‖‖‖
Given our resources and relationships and faith, how many people do you think we could help emancipate in the next 12 months?

- What do you think it would take to make that happen?

REFLECTION

> Take five quiet minutes to consider this list of things people are already doing to challenge oppression around the world (I'll let you know at the three minute point): **[handout]**

‖‖‖
Paying Attention.

- They watch reliable national and international news media and web sites for clues about what's happening in the world and how they can act for justice.

‖‖‖
Praying.

- They talk to God about justice specifically and relentlessly.

THE JUSTICE MISSION

3

||||
Giving.

- They fund the justice work of organizations like International Justice Mission;

- They give to the justice missions of their churches;

||||
Telling Stories.

- Whatever they learn about justice, they teach to anyone willing to learn;

- They talk with church leaders about supporting justice missions;

- They talk with law enforcement professionals, officers of the court and diplomats about the justice-making activities of agencies like International Justice Mission.

||||
Crossing Borders.

- They choose careers that cross borders to challenge injustice and oppression

[FOR MORE ON CROSS-CULTURAL CAREER PATHS GO TO IJM.ORG/JUSTICEMISSION]

||||
Now answer these questions:

- How can I pay more attention?
- How can I pray?
- What can I give?
- How can I become a justice storyteller?
- Can I prepare to fight injustice across borders?

ACTION

||||
Pray: Ask God this week how you can join the fight against injustice.

- If this all seems a little overwhelming, consider this prayer from Reinhold Neibuhr **[handout]**

> *God, grant me the serenity*
> *to accept the things I cannot change,*
> *the courage to change the things I can,*
> *and the wisdom to know the difference.*
> *Living one day at a time,*
> *enjoying one moment at a time;*
> *accepting hardship as a pathway to peace;*
> *taking, as Jesus did,*
> *this sinful world as it is,*
> *not as I would have it;*
> *trusting that You will make all things right*
> *if I surrender to your will;*
> *so that I may be reasonably happy in this life*
> *and supremely happy*
> *with You forever in the next.*
> *Amen*

Looking at the injustice we're talking about, where do you need serenity?

- Ask God for serenity this week to accept the circumstances you absolutely can't do anything about.

Where do you need courage to resist oppressors?

- Ask God for courage to act against injustice wherever you find it this week.

Where do you need wisdom to see the difference between what you can change and what you can't?

- Ask God for what you need.

▌▌▌▌
Website: Go to <u>IJM.org/Justice Mission</u> for more on God's call to join the fight for justice. Here are other web sources:

Amnesty International, www.amnesty.org
Children's Defense Fund, www.childrensdefense.org
Compassion International, www.compassion.com
Evangelicals for Social Action, www.esa-online.org
Human Rights Watch, www.hrw.org
U2, U2.com

▌▌▌▌
Dig: Interview someone who fights injustice in law enforcement or community organizing or ministry to oppressed people (find someone in your community or get the e-mail addresses of a missionary your church supports and conduct an internet interview).

Find out:
- how they got started.
- what their challenges are.
- what keeps them going when times are hard.

▌▌▌▌
Funding: get with some friends and see if you can figure out how to raise enough money this week ($500 U.S.) to free one person from bonded labor.

▌▌▌▌
Journal: At least every other day this week, write about what you're seeing, hearing and feeling about God's call to create justice for the oppressed. **[handout]**

Let's finish by asking God how we should join the fight for justice.

1. Take five quiet minutes to consider this list of things people are already doing to challenge oppression around the world

Paying Attention.

- They watch reliable national and international news media and web sites for clues about what's happening in the world and how they can act for justice.

Praying.

- They talk to God about justice specifically and relentlessly.

Giving.

- They fund the justice work of organizations like International Justice Mission;
- They give to the justice missions of their churches;

Telling Stories.

- Whatever they learn about justice, they teach to anyone willing to learn;
- They talk with church leaders about supporting justice missions;
- They talk with law enforcement professionals, officers of the court and diplomats about the justice-making activities of agencies like International Justice Mission.

Crossing Borders.

- They choose careers that cross borders to challenge injustice and oppression
[FOR MORE ON CROSS-CULTURAL CAREER PATHS GO TO IJM.ORG/JUSTICEMISSION]

THE JUSTICE MISSION

2. Now answer these questions:

SESSION 3

a. How can I pay more attention?

b. How can I pray?

c. What can I give?

d. How can I become a justice storyteller?

e. Can I prepare to fight injustice across borders?

What new thoughts have you had
ABOUT GOD in the time we've been
working on the Justice Mission?

What new insights have you had
ABOUT YOURSELF in the time
we've been working on the Justice
Mission?

3

3

What could keep you from raising 500 bucks to R E S C U E someone from bonded slavery?

What could you do to O V E R C O M E those obstacles?

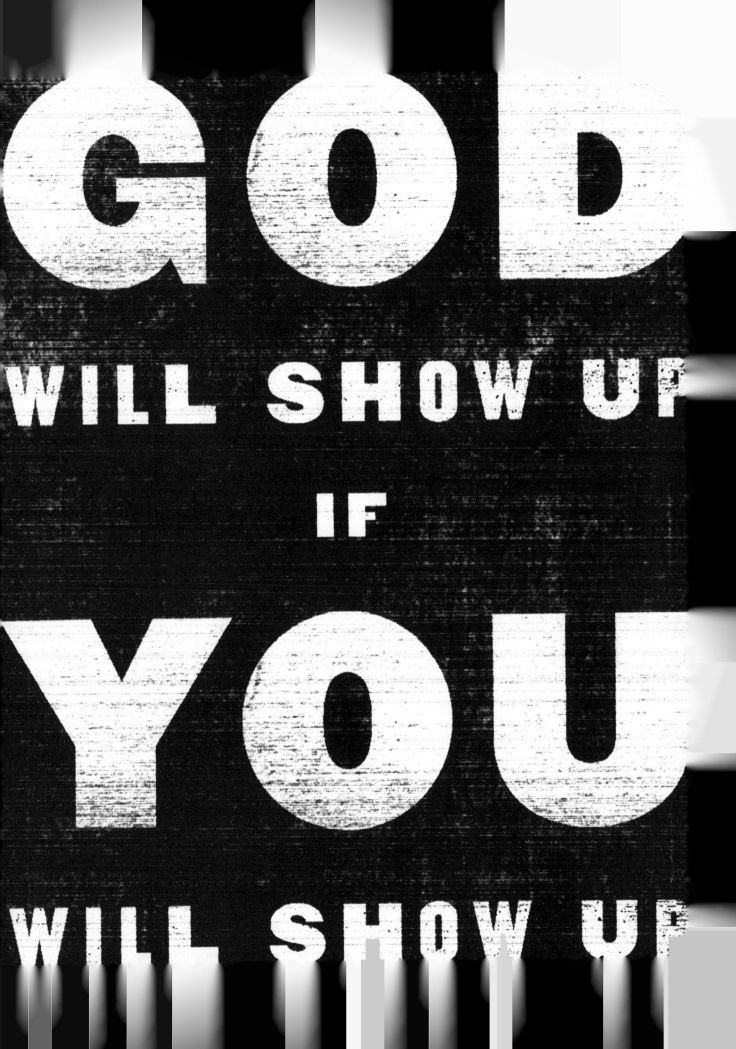

GOD
WILL SHOW UP
IF
YOU
WILL SHOW UP

THE JUSTICE MISSION 4
GOD'S VISION BRINGS GOD'S PROVISION

STUFF

- Newsprint, crayons, magazines, scissors, glue sticks, Play-Doh; Bibles; response lists; blank paper and pencils; video playback and Justice Mission video cued to *The Justice Mission* segment.

GATHERING

- **Art Project:** create images of Justice

OPERATING INSTRUCTIONS

- **Bible Study:** John 6:1-21

THE BIG IDEA

- **Video-driven discussion:** The Justice Mission

REFLECTION

- **Instruction & Group Inventory:** counting the costs and resources in the fight for justice

ACTION

- **Action:** Pray

- **Website:** IJM web site

- **Journal:** Personal Journaling

THIS SESSION

We spend a lot time in this culture—not you, probably, but schools and parents and employers do—reminding kids they're only kids. Then we criticize them for failing to think original thoughts, failing to resist the devil, failing to make the world a better place to live. Shame on us.

God's story on planet earth is full of tales about kids doing great things. Truly: how many times have you admonished students with Paul's words to Timothy? "Don't let anyone look down on you because you are young, but set an example for the believers in speech, in life, in love, in faith and in purity."

This session is about letting your group know you're convinced God will show up if they show up; God will take whatever they give and multiply it 5,000 times so it's big enough to put a serious dent in oppression; God will never ever use the word *only* in the same sentence with the word *kid*.

Do you believe that? If you don't, confess it. If you do, *sell it.*

GATHERING

 What did you learn about oppression and justice this week?

> Help yourself to supplies and create images that show justice overcoming oppression—no rules, don't overthink it; just see what comes out your fingers.

[INVITE EVERYONE TO DISPLAY THEIR ART ON A TABLE TOP OR WALL.]

 What strikes you about these works of art?

- If you see something that gives you fresh ideas about creating justice, please point it out to us.

OPERATING INSTRUCTIONS

> Let's read John 6:1-21.

> Following a particularly spirited encounter with his critics—at the end of which they really wanted him dead—Jesus moved on to greener pastures (as it were)

1 Some time after this, Jesus crossed to the far shore of the Sea of Galilee (that is, the Sea of Tiberias),

2 and a great crowd of people followed him because they saw the miraculous signs he had performed on the sick.

3 Then Jesus went up on a mountainside and sat down with his disciples.

4 The Jewish Passover Feast was near.

5 When Jesus looked up and saw a great crowd coming toward him, he said to Philip, "Where shall we buy bread for these people to eat?"

6 He asked this only to test him, for he already had in mind what he was going to do.

[INTERRUPT THE READING HERE]

It's a trick question! Got the picture? Middle of nowhere? Huge hungry crowd? "Where shall we buy bread for these people?" is a trick question! Jesus already knows what he's going to do.

? Do you believe that about injustice? Do you believe Jesus already knows what he's going to do about injustice? Why?

- If we agree for the moment that Jesus probably already has a plan in place, why do you think he bothers to bring us into it?

Let's pick up at verse seven to hear Philip's response.

7 Philip answered him, "Eight months' wages would not buy enough bread for each one to have a bite!"

[INTERRUPT AGAIN.]

? What do you think Philip is feeling at this point?

? Think about injustice: What do you think it will cost to create justice in the world?

- Can we afford it? Because...

Verse eight:

8 Another of his disciples, Andrew, Simon Peter's brother, spoke up,

9 "Here is a boy with five small barley loaves and two small fish, but how far will they go among so many?"

[INTERRUPT AGAIN.]

A drop in the bucket; spit in the ocean; a Kid's Meal. Why even bother?

? Do you ever think that about your resources for fighting injustice? Do you ever say, "Hey, I'm only a kid"?

Now watch what Jesus does. Verse ten:

10 Jesus said, "Have the people sit down." There was plenty of grass in that place, and the men sat down, about five thousand of them.

11 Jesus then took the loaves, gave thanks, and distributed to those who were seated as much as they wanted. He did the same with the fish.

12 When they had all had enough to eat, he said to his disciples, "Gather the pieces that are left over. Let nothing be wasted."

[INTERRUPT]

Think for a moment about the way Jesus acted here. He took the child's lunch; he gave thanks, he distributed as much as each person wanted...

And, as if by magic, they all had enough—5,000 of them.

? Why are there hungry people in the world?

- Do you believe there's enough food for everyone? It's a fundamental question: *scarcity* or *abundance*. If you believe in scarcity, you have to hoard because there may not be enough to go around; if you believe in abundance, you can afford to be generous because there's plenty. Perhaps it just hasn't been distributed effectively.

? How would you say you've lived your life: believing in *scarcity* or *abundance*?

- How has that worked out for you emotionally, spiritually and relationally so far? (Here's a hint: generosity is about abundance, stinginess and greed are about scarcity)

? Do you believe there's enough justice to go around? Why?

? Was there—in grocery store terms—enough food for all those people?

- What did that kid's food have to do with feeding all those folks?

What do you have in your hand that God could miraculously transform into enough justice for everyone at the picnic? a little knowledge? a little anger? a little passion? a little influence? a few relationships? a bit of freedom to decide what you'll study and how you'll try to spend the rest of your life?

[INDICATE FIVE PLACES IN THE ROOM THAT REPRESENT A CONTINUUM FROM ONE TO FIVE. IF YOU WANT TO KEEP THEM IN ONE PLACE, HAVE FOLKS STAND ON THEIR CHAIR FOR FIVE, STAND ON THE FLOOR FOR FOUR, SIT ON THE CHAIR FOR THREE, KNEEL FOR TWO AND SIT ON THE FLOOR FOR ONE.]

After each statement, please go stand on the spot that represents your attitude. One means you strongly disagree, five means you strongly agree, two, three or four means you're not fully persuaded.

IIIII

I have a little *knowledge* God can use to fight injustice.

IIIII

I have a little *anger* God can use to end oppression.

IIIII

I have a little *passion* God can guide to help the helpless.

IIIII

I have a little *influence* God can use to involve others in the search for justice.

IIIII

I have a few *relationships* God can energize to create a team of people committed to changing the world as we know it.

IIIII

I have a bit of *freedom* to decide what I'll study and how I'll spend the rest of my life.

God takes a little and turns it into a lot. Here's the big finish, starting with verse 13:

13 So they gathered them and filled twelve baskets with the pieces of the five barley loaves left over by those who had eaten.

[INTERRUPT]

Not just enough. More than enough. Let's keep going:

14 After the people saw the miraculous sign that Jesus did, they began to say, "Surely this is the Prophet who is to come into the world."

15 Jesus, knowing that they intended to come and make him king by force, withdrew again to a mountain by himself.

16 When evening came, his disciples went down to the lake,

17 where they got into a boat and set off across the lake for Capernaum. By now it was dark, and Jesus had not yet joined them.

18 A strong wind was blowing and the waters grew rough.

19 When they had rowed three or three and a half miles, they saw Jesus approaching the boat, walking on the water; and they were terrified.

20 But he said to them, "It is I; don't be afraid."

21 Then they were willing to take him into the boat, and immediately the boat reached the shore where they were heading.

? How do you imagine Jesus' disciples felt when the crowd wanted to make him king (whether he wanted it or not)?

- How do you think they felt a few hours later when it looked like they might be lost at sea?

Mark tells the end of the story just a little differently in Mark 6:51,52

---

51 Then he climbed into the boat with them, and the wind died down. They were completely amazed,

52 for they had not understood about the loaves; their hearts were hardened.

"...they had not understood about the loaves; their hearts were hardened."

? What do you think hardens peoples' hearts to the work of God?

- Do you think your heart has been hard about how God intends to rescue victims of oppression?

- Have you failed to understand what Jesus is capable of doing through the small gifts of powerless people?

[IF YOU HAVE TIME, LOOK AT 1 CORINTHIANS 1:26-31 AND ROMANS 8:26-28. IF NOT, SKIP DOWN TO THE VIDEO.]

Let's look at 1 Corinthians 1:26-31.

---

26 Brothers, think of what you were when you were called. Not many of you were wise by human standards; not many were influential; not many were of noble birth.

[INTERRUPT]

? Does this sound like anyone you know?

- Do any of these fit you?

Pick it up again at verse 27:

---

27 But God chose the foolish things of the world to shame the wise; God chose the weak things of the world to shame the strong.

4

THE JUSTICE MISSION

28 He chose the lowly things of this world and the despised things—and the things that are not—to nullify the things that are,

29 so that no one may boast before him.

30 It is because of him that you are in Christ Jesus, who has become for us wisdom from God—that is, our righteousness, holiness and redemption.

31 Therefore, as it is written: "Let him who boasts boast in the Lord."

? Realistically, what do you think people like us can accomplish to create justice in the world?

  ● If you haven't already, add God to the equation. How does your answer change? Why?

> Robert Murray McCheyne said, "If I could hear Christ praying for me in the next room, I would not fear a million enemies. Yet distance makes no difference, as He is praying for me."

Jesus is nearer than the next room and your name is on His lips. As Hebrews 7:25 puts it, Jesus is able to save completely those who come to God through Him, because He always lives to intercede for them.

> Romans 8: 26-39 picks up the thread:

26 In the same way, the Spirit helps us in our weakness. We do not know what we ought to pray for, but the Spirit himself intercedes for us with groans that words cannot express.

27 And he who searches our hearts knows the mind of the Spirit, because the Spirit intercedes for the saints in accordance with God's will.

28 And we know that in all things God works for the good of those who love him, who have been called according to his purpose.

? If you find it difficult to believe, that's fair enough, but is there any question in your mind that the Bible says God is there for people like us, ready to do amazing things we could never imagine doing on our own?

  ● Talk about that.

THE BIG IDEA

> I want to show you a video called *The Justice Mission.*

[AS THE VIDEO SEGMENT ENDS:]

? What stands out for you in that video?

- Why do you think that's significant?

- What ideas does that give you about your own next steps?

? Lindsay, Bob, and Gary talked about all the ways a person can prepare to do justice. How many do you remember?

[THEY INCLUDED INVESTIGATORS, LAWYERS, LAW ENFORCEMENT PROFESSIONALS, COPS, PRAYER PARTNERS, GOVERNMENT RELATIONS PEOPLE, DIPLOMATS, LETTER WRITERS (WRITING TO MEMBERS OF CONGRESS AND SENATORS), STORYTELLERS, AND—ALTHOUGH THEY DIDN'T USE THIS TERM—INFLUENCERS WHO MOBILIZE A NETWORK OF RELATIONSHIPS BY TELLING THE TRUTH ABOUT OPPRESSION AND INJUSTICE WHEREVER THEY FIND IT.]

- Does that list make you more hopeful or more fearful? Talk about that.

? Ben said, "I realized the people who were going to read that and do something about it was us." How do you think that applies to our situation?

? Do you have a sense of what God may be asking you to do in response to what you're learning about injustice in the world?

- On a scale of one to five (with five being very hard) how hard is it for you to believe God can use your resources to overcome injustice?

? Trever said, "I've heard the saying that, 'If this were easy, everyone would be doing it.' I honestly think I want to be one of those people who does it anyway." If that's true for you as well, would you just stand up where you are [OR RAISE YOUR HAND OR WHATEVER YOU THINK IS APPROPRIATE] *?*

Before we go on, just reach out and grab a hand or touch the people near you. I want to ask God to help us figure out what we ought to do about justice and how to do it.

[AFTER YOU PRAY, CONTINUE WITH THE RESOURCES BELOW.]

There are four important, and perhaps unexpected, resources for fighting oppression, even when it's hard to believe:[1]

Walk Humbly with God

- What does the Lord require of you? To do justice, to love mercy, to walk humbly with your God. Followers of Jesus are called to fight oppression from a position of humble dependence on God, not from self-righteous indignation. We are called to be rescuers, not saviors—that position is already filled.

? Are you more likely to follow the lead of someone who strikes you as arrogant or someone who seems humble? Why is that?

---

1 adopted from Gary A. Haugen, Good News About Injustice, 1999, Downers Grove, InterVarsity Press p. 113-118.

|||||
Remember the Incarnation

- God is not napping while oppressors wreak havoc on the earth. God came among us in Jesus Christ to endure the full force of oppression. Jesus defeated injustice forever by his resurrection from the grave. Compared to that, what we're doing now is a mopping-up exercise.

That's not to say oppressed people aren't really oppressed; it's just to acknowledge that, in the end, we believe the good news is about twice as good as the bad news is bad. God is with us in Jesus Christ.

? Luke 4:16-21 records one of Jesus' first public statements. He says "The Spirit of the Lord is on me, because he has anointed me to preach good news to the poor. He has sent me to proclaim freedom for the prisoners and recovery of sight for the blind, to release the oppressed, to proclaim the year of the Lord's favor." How does his self-description match the descriptions of Jesus you've grown up with?

- What does that tell you?

|||||
Love God

- Loving God with all your heart and soul and mind and strength is half the answer Jesus gave when a seeker asked about the greatest commandment. The other half is loving your neighbor as you love yourself. It's a big idea. Before Jesus, no one combined those halves into one holy obligation.

Loving God leads to godly obedience more surely than guilt ever did. Learn to love God truly and you'll learn to truly love what God loves and truly hate what God hates. Love God and then—to paraphrase St. Augustine—do what comes naturally.

? Do you find it easier to make and follow through with commitments motivated by guilt or commitments motivated by love?

- What does that suggest to you?

|||||
Keep One Eye on the Horizon

- Just beyond what we can see with our eyes is life with God forever. It's the old pie-in-the-sky thing: Christians have a long (if imperfect) history of sacrificing comfortable living in the short term because we believe there's an endless supply of comfort in the not-too-distant future. As Jim Elliot wrote in college: "One of the great blessings of Heaven is the appreciation of heaven on earth... He is no fool who gives what he cannot keep, to gain that which he cannot lose."[2]

The promise of eternal life is the hope that anything we sacrifice on earth will be generously compensated in the Land Beyond Time.

---

[2] www.wheaton.edu/bgc/archives/faq/20.htm

? Think carefully about this: Do you think you could sacrifice some of your life expectations in the short term if you knew you'd get a hundred times more in heaven?

- What hopes for your future are most difficult for you to consider sacrificing? Why is that?
- How many self-sacrificing Christians do you think it would take to end oppression for good?

REFLECTION

Write a letter to God. **[handout]**

ACTION

||||||

Pray: Ask God this week how you can join the fight against injustice.

- If you don't know what to pray, here's a prayer adapted from The Book of Common Prayer.[3] **[handout]**

  Grant, O God, that your holy, life-giving Spirit may so move our hearts that we may learn to love what you love and hate what you hate because we love you with our whole heart and mind and strength.

  God, you have bound us together in a common struggle for justice and truth. Nurture in us a love for our neighbors like your love for us. Strengthen us to bring down every injustice, every form of oppression, every evil scheme and to establish justice and peace.

  Almighty and merciful God, we remember before you all poor and neglected persons whom it would be easy for us to forget. Look with pity, heavenly Father, on all who live with injustice, terror, disease and death as their constant companions. Have mercy on us for what we have left undone in the fight for justice. Help us eliminate all cruelty to these our neighbors that we all may share in the abundance of your creation.

  Strengthen those who spend their lives establishing equal protection under the law and equal opportunity for every person. Grant that every person, whoever she is and wherever she lives, may enjoy a fair portion of the riches of the earth.

  Almighty God, you sit on your throne judging right and wrong: bless the courts of justice and the magistrates in every nation; give them the spirit of wisdom and understanding that, fearing you alone they may discern the truth, and impartially administer the law.

---

[3]http://justus.anglican.org/resources/bcp/bcp.htm

God, you have called us to yourself. Now draw us into your service to pursue justice and peace, healing all who are broken in body or spirit, turning their sorrow into joy. Grant this Father, for the love of your Son, who for our sake was oppressed and unjustly executed; our Savior and Judge; our righteousness and peace; Jesus Christ, our resurrected Lord.

||||||
Website: Go to IJM.org/JusticeMission for more on God's provision for fighting oppression and creating justice.

||||||
Funding: get with some friends and see if you can figure out how to raise enough money this week ($1000 US) to free one person from sexual slavery.

||||||
Journal: At least every other day this week, write about what you're seeing, hearing and feeling about God's call to create justice for the oppressed. [**handout**]

Let's finish by praying the prayer on the handout again.

THE JUSTICE MISSION

Walking Humbly with God

Keeping One Eye on the Horizon

Remembering the Incarnation

Loving God

---

1. In which of these do you feel strongest right now?

Why is that?

2. In which of these do you feel weakest right now?

Why is that?

3. What do you think you can contribute to your group out of that strength?

4. What do you think your group can do to help you in that weakness?

THE JUSTICE MISSION

SESSION

4

What resources—however small or large—can you offer to God
in the FIGHT to create justice for oppressed people?

How do you feel about considering a career in LAW
ENFORCEMENT or DIPLOMATIC RELATIONS or
some other work to pursue justice? Does that idea generate dread
or excitement in you?

What could keep you from raising a thousand bucks to RESCUE SOMEONE from forced prostitution?

4

THE JUSTICE MISSION

What could you do to OVERCOME those obstacles?

5

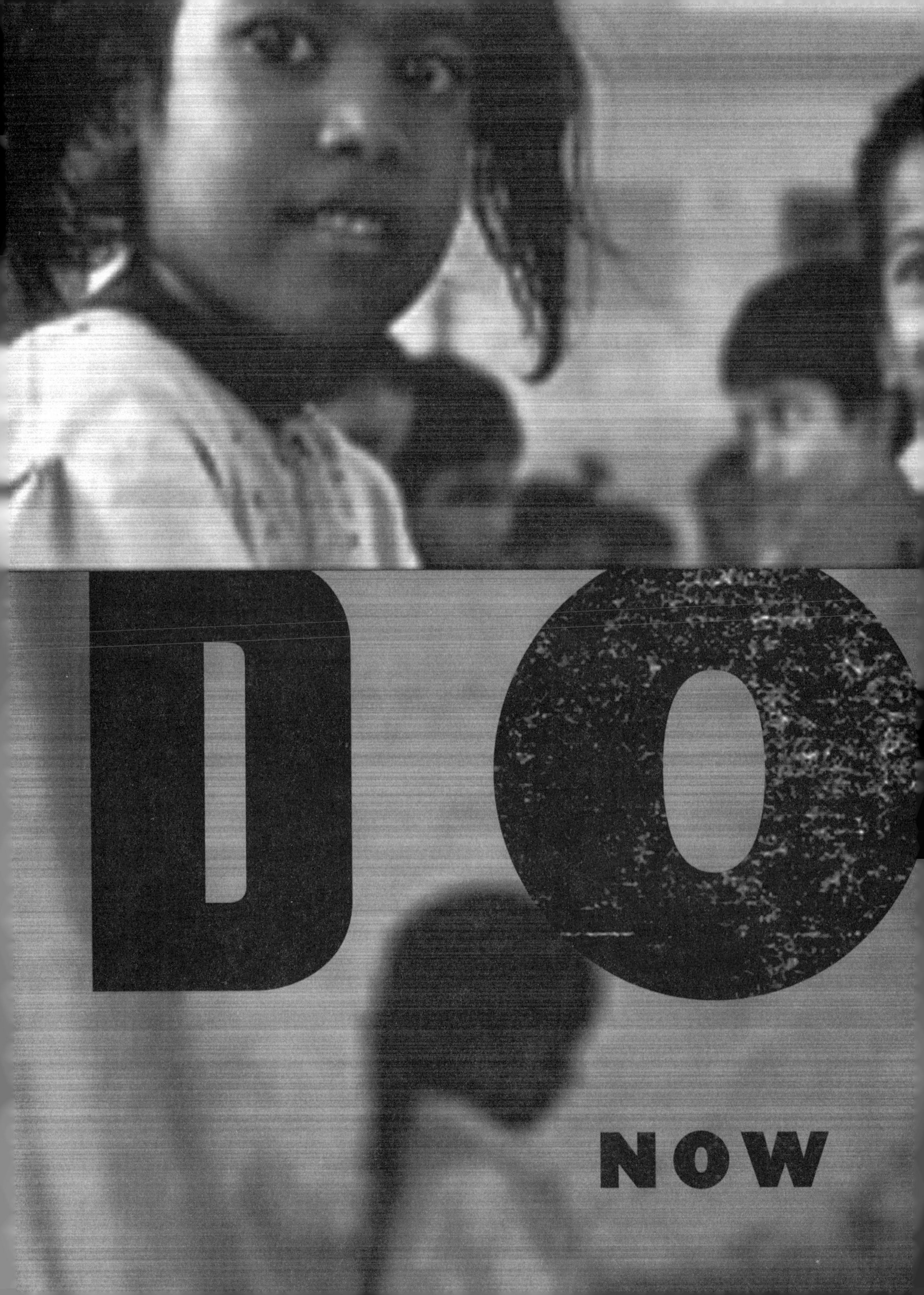
D O
NOW

THE JUSTICE MISSION 5
DO IT NOW

STUFF

- Bibles; blank paper and pencils; video playback and *Justice Mission* video cued to *Rescue.*

GATHERING

- **Show and Tell:** Group Reflection on the *Justice Mission* high points.

VIDEO

- **Video-driven discussion:** *Rescue*

OPERATING INSTRUCTIONS

- **Bible Study:** James 1:22-27

THE BIG IDEA

- **Imagination and group decision-making**

REFLECTION

- **Write a note to God**

ACTION

- **WebSight:** Go to IJM.org/JusticeMission to tell them about your experience with the Justice Mission and find out what you can do next.

- **Organize:** get with some friends and begin organizing your action steps.

- **Journal:** At least every other day this week, write about what you're seeing, hearing and feeling about God's call to create justice for the oppressed.

THIS SESSION

Sustainability is the gold standard in learning—that's true in every area, isn't it? I mean, who makes you more nervous, the student who knows nothing about God when you begin, or the one who knows way more than she's done anything about? Sorry, that's a rhetorical question and I promised I wouldn't do that.

Nothing about the Justice Mission is in order to *know* something about creating justice, it's all in order to *do* something (and keep doing something) about creating justice.

This session is where that begins in earnest. If you've already had success raising money to rescue a person trapped in bonded labor or forced prostitution, you're already moving; if not, this session will help you get the ball rolling. It's no secret we hope a big part of that involves the International Justice Mission.

Just so you know, here's how IJM spends the money youth groups raise.

IJM FINDS people who are victims of oppressors through an international network of relationships with NGOs[1]

IJM INVESTIGATES the claims made by victims against their oppressors.

IJM DOCUMENTS the legal case against oppressors.

IJM FILES the legal case with duly constituted authorities and continues to monitor and refile the case until someone takes action in favor of the victims.

IJM RESCUES victims where doing so hastens their release.

IJM FUNDS aftercare partners to ensure that rescued people have a fresh start.[2]

IJM PROSECUTES oppressors whenever possible to put them out of business for good.

Put all that together and IJM very nearly defines sustainability.

Which is why we hope you'll decide to enter a long term relationship with IJM (and by we, I mean Youth Specialties and me). We hope you'll become a partner in creating justice in the world. We hope you'll deputize students to explore justice-making careers. We hope you'll infect your organization and relational web with the justice virus. We hope when you die from natural causes at the end of a long stretch as a youth worker you will have just absent-mindedly remarked for the second time in less than a month, "You know, there was a brief period when Christians forgot how to do justice...aren't you glad we got *that* squared away?"

If that happens, we will have achieved sustainability.

---

[1] Non-Governmental Organizations (NGOs) include missionary boards, relief missions, development agencies, medical societies and the like. NGO's are known to the government in the countries where they operate (they didn't sneak across the border) and their work is generally welcomed by government officials.

[2] IJM funds the immediate aftercare of individuals they rescue. IJM's aftercare partners continue the process from there. Aftercare partners include local congregations and outside relief and development agencies. Find out more about IJM's aftercare partners on the web at IJM.org/JusticeMission.

GATHERING

Show and Tell

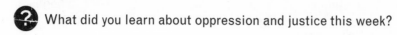

? What did you learn about oppression and justice this week?

? If someone asked what we've been working on the last few weeks, how would you describe it to them?

- What would you tell them is the most significant thing you've learned in this process?
- If they asked why you think that's important, what would you say?

- And if they said, "Well, that's interesting, but what do you plan to do about it?" How would you answer?

VIDEO: RESCUE

? I want to show you a video called *Rescue.* You already know part of this story, but you haven't seen it from this point of view.

[AS THE VIDEO ENDS, ASK:]

? What stands out for you in Jyothi's story?

- Is there anything you caught this time that you missed before?

> What Jyothi knew about her rescue is that she prayed and a week later Bob showed up, looking like any other customer but planning to get her out of the brothel.

What she didn't know is all the steps along the way. Here is how IJM works:

IJM FINDS people who are victims of oppressors through an international network of relationships with Non-Governmental Organizations. NGOs include missionary boards, relief missions, development agencies, medical societies and the like. NGOs are known to the government in the countries where they operate (they didn't sneak across the border) and their work is generally welcomed by government officials. The woman who told Jyothi about Jesus is part of the IJM network.

IJM INVESTIGATES the claims made by victims against their oppressors.

IJM DOCUMENTS the legal case against oppressors.

IJM FILES the legal case within duly constituted authorities and continues to monitor and refile the case until someone takes action in favor of the victims.

IJM RESCUES victims where doing so hastens their release.

IJM FUNDS the immediate aftercare of individuals they rescue. IJM's aftercare partners continue the process from there. Aftercare partners include local congregations and outside relief and development agencies. Jyothi was placed in a home operated by an aftercare partner.

 Jyothi said she prays for girls like her who are held against their will as sex slaves. And she asked us to do the same thing. Would someone be willing to take a moment to pray right now for girls trapped in forced prostitution?

[AFTER YOU'VE PRAYED, CONTINUE WITH THE BIBLE-DRIVEN DISCUSSION BELOW.]

OPERATING INSTRUCTIONS

> Let's read James 1:22-27

22 Do not merely listen to the word, and so deceive yourselves. Do what it says.

23 Anyone who listens to the word but does not do what it says is like a man who looks at his ace in a mirror

24 and, after looking at himself, goes away and immediately forgets what he looks like.

25 But the man who looks intently into the perfect law that gives freedom, and continues to do this, not forgetting what he has heard, but doing it—he will be blessed in what he does.

26 If anyone considers himself religious and yet does not keep a tight rein on his tongue, he deceives himself and his religion is worthless.

27 Religion that God our Father accepts as pure and faultless is this: to look after orphans and widows in their distress and to keep oneself from being polluted by the world.

 What stands out for you in this passage?

- Why do you think that's important?

 Why do you think we chose this passage for our last Bible Study in the *Justice Mission?*

 In what ways has this Justice Mission series been a mirror for you?

- Have you been surprised (pleasantly or unpleasantly) by anything you've seen in this process?

 What could keep you from remembering what you saw in the mirror?

- What can we do for each other to make sure that doesn't happen?

THE BIG IDEA

Imagine

[DISTRIBUTE PAPER AND PENCILS]

> I'd like you to imagine something with me. It starts with a list of your friends

IIIII
Name your closest circle of friends, however small or large that is. If you don't have both boys and girls on your list, add the name of a brother or sister or close relative. Circle the name of one male and one female.

IIIII
Now imagine you all are poor, living in a rural community where you never see a police officer, the nearest courthouse is 50 miles away, and you don't even know anyone who owns a motorized vehicle.

IIIII
Imagine the two people whose names you circled are in the sort of bind we've been learning about—he stops coming to school because he got trapped in bonded labor, and she drops out of sight for month before you find out she's been kidnapped and forced into sexual slavery. How do you think you'd feel about that?

IIIII
Imagine now that, through no credit of your own, you and your friends are suddenly transported to the life you have now—*you* get to live where you live, go to your school, shop, eat, do all the thing you normally do.

...Except for your two friends who are caught in the grip of oppressors. They're still stuck where they were. How do you think you'd feel about that?

IIIII
Now imagine you meet a group that specializes in getting the legal system to release people from bonded labor and forced prostitution, and they can do it for 500 or a thousand bucks. How would you respond to that?

IIIII
If all this were true, what do you think you and the rest of your friends would do to get the thousand dollars or 500 dollars to rescue the two in trouble? Be specific; is this bake sales and car washes or does it take something more urgent to rescue friends in this kind of trouble?

IIIII
How long would you wait? How long would it take you and your friends to get started if you knew $500 or $1000 would get your friends back where they belong?

 Do you see where this is going? What's your reaction to this line of thought?

[STARTING NOW, HAVE SOMEONE WRITE BIG IDEAS ON BUTCHER PAPER OR INDIVIDUAL SHEETS OF PAPER AND PLACE THEM ON THE WALLS FOR LATER.]

A couple of sessions back we saw what other people are doing to challenge oppression.

|||||
They *pay attention* to reliable media around the world.

? If you're doing more of that, more intentionally, tell us something you've gotten in touch with in the process.

|||||
They *pray,* talking with God specifically and often.

? If you're praying more about injustice, tell us something you've gotten in touch with in the process.

|||||
They *give* to groups like International Justice Mission who focus on doing justice.

? If you've given money recently to help create justice, tell us something you've gotten in touch with in the process.

|||||
They *tell stories* about doing justice to people in their network of relationships.

? If you've told stories recently to get others interested in doing justice, tell us something you've gotten in touch with in the process.

|||||
They *cross borders* to do justice in their working lives.

? If you've considered a justice-making career, tell us something you've gotten in touch with in the process.

? What can we do to sharpen the way we pay attention to those who pay attention to justice?

? What can we start doing to help us pray more intelligently and persistently about justice?

? What can we do to raise serious money for rescues? Let's brainstorm as many ideas as we can in three minutes. **[WRITE THESE DOWN, HOWEVER BIZARRE THEY MAY SEEM AT THE MOMENT—THE STUPID IDEAS WILL GO AWAY ON THEIR OWN OR BE REPLACED BY BETTER ONES.]**

? Who needs to know what we've been learning about justice?

|||||
Let's make a list of groups and influencers we could try to get involved in doing justice.

[SALT THE LIST-MAKING WITH QUESTIONS TO GET YOUR GROUP THINKING ABOUT VARIOUS ADULT GATHERINGS, OTHER YOUTH GROUPS, PARENTS, LAW ENFORCE-MENT GROUPS, CHURCH AND ORGANIZATIONAL BOARDS, FOUNDATIONS]

[FOR EACH INDIVIDUAL OR GROUP ON YOUR LIST...]

|||||
What can we use to help them get the picture?

- If they agreed to give us one hour (and maybe they'd give us more after that) what videos, Bible Studies, discussions and stories would you want to use?

Let's not forget where we live. What do you think we ought to do about closer-range injustice right here?

|||||
What can we do in your school?

|||||
What can we do in the neighborhood right around us?

|||||
What can we do in the larger community?

Is there anything you would add to this list?

We have a lot of a possibilities.

- What are the obstacles to the action we're planning?

- Who can help us?

> When I say, "go," please move around the room with your pencil and put your name next to anything you'd be interested in helping with. We'll just take a couple of minutes now; you can spend some more time on it after we close. I'll compile the lists and someone will contact you in the next few days about the next step. Are you ready? All right, go ahead.

REFLECTION

> Write a note to God about what you just decided to get involved with. Tell God what you want to do and ask for the resources to get it done.

> As we finish, let's pray Psalm 103 together.

1 Praise the LORD, O my soul; all my inmost being, praise his holy name.

2 Praise the LORD, O my soul, and forget not all his benefits—

3 who forgives all your sins and heals all your diseases,

4 who redeems your life from the pit and crowns you with love and compassion,

5 who satisfies your desires with good things so that your youth is renewed like the eagle's.

THE JUSTICE MISSION *(vertical left margin)*

6 The LORD works righteousness and justice for all the oppressed.

7 He made known his ways to Moses, his deeds to the people of Israel:

8 The LORD is compassionate and gracious, slow to anger, abounding in love.

9 He will not always accuse, nor will he harbor his anger forever;

10 he does not treat us as our sins deserve or repay us according to our iniquities.

11 For as high as the heavens are above the earth, so great is his love for those who fear him;

12 as far as the east is from the west, so far has he removed our transgressions from us.

13 As a father has compassion on his children, so the LORD has compassion on those who fear him;

14 for he knows how we are formed, he remembers that we are dust.

15 As for man, his days are like grass, he flourishes like a flower of the field;

16 the wind blows over it and it is gone, and its place remembers it no more.

17 But from everlasting to everlasting the LORD'S love is with those who fear him, and his righteousness with their children's children—

18 with those who keep his covenant and remember to obey his precepts.

19 The LORD has established his throne in heaven, and his kingdom rules over all.

20 Praise the LORD, you his angels, you mighty ones who do his bidding, who obey his word.

21 Praise the LORD, all his heavenly hosts, you his servants who do his will.

22 Praise the LORD, all his works everywhere in his dominion. Praise the LORD, O my soul.

> In the same spirit, let's thank God for all we're learning and ask for energy and imagination to keep fighting oppression in the name of Jesus. Pray out loud when you're ready, or silently if you prefer.

JOURNALING

[handout]

This week...

||||
Website: Go to IJM.org/JusticeMission to tell them about your experience with the Justice Mission and find out what you can do next.

||||
Organize: get with some friends and begin organizing your action steps.

||||
Journal: At least every other day this week, write about what you're seeing, hearing and feeling about God's call to create justice for the oppressed.

||||
What's the most important insight you've had about God in this process? Why is that so important?

||||

What's the most significant insight you had into your own life and faith in this process? Why is that important? What do you want to do about it?

||||

Who is likely to be an ally in your plans to do justice? What could you ask them to do to help you follow through with your intentions?

||||

Try summarizing what you've learned about doing justice in fewer than 100 words.

WORKSHEET

Write a note to God about what you just decided to get involved with. Tell God what you want to do and ask for the resources to get it done.

THE JUSTICE MISSION

SESSION

5

What's the most important
insight you've had
ABOUT GOD in this
process? Why is that so
important?

Who is likely to be an ally in your
plans to do justice? What could you
ask them to do to help you follow
through with your intentions?

This week:
WEBSITE:
Go to IJM.org/
JusticeMission to tell
them about your
experience with the
Justice Mission and
find out what you can
do next.
ORGANIZE:
get with some friends
and begin organizing
your action steps.
JOURNAL:
At least every other
day this week, write
about what you're see-
ing, hearing and
feeling about God's
call to create justice
for the oppressed.

5

Try summarizing what you've
learned about DOING justice in
fewer than 100 words.

What's the most significant insight you
had into your own LIFE AND
FAITH in this process? Why is that
important? What do you want to do
about it?

5

abusive child labor

child pornography

abusive military action

intimidation

racial or ethnic violence

corruption of ju

detaining without lawful
charge or trial

injustice
oppression
abuse of power
it's none of my business

I don't know those people
they're not bothering me

even if they were...
I'm just a kid.
cut me some slack here

sex slaves
widows
 orphans
bonded labor
cops killing street kids
forced relocation
kidnapping

what am I supposed to do
about that?
you want me to feel bad?
fine. I feel bad.

now what?

it's halfway around the world and
I'm just a kid
If it's so important
why haven't our parents fixed it already

I don't get it
I mean, really
isn't that what God is
supposed to do?

I'm sympathetic and all
but really?
I don't see how that stuff is any

of my business

even if it were...
I'm just a kid.
(I guess I said that already)

I'm just a kid

I'm just a kid

I'm just a kid

I'm just a kid

look
i don't wanna feel bad
i want to feel useful
gimme something i can do

just help me to understand
if there's something to be done
i'll do it

if i thought i could actually make a difference
if i really believed God had a plan—
and it was me—
nothing could stop me.

I'm just a kid

THE L

WO

RIGHTE

JUS

FOR THE

ORD

RKS

USNESS&

TICE

PPRESSED

RESOURCES FROM YOUTH SPECIALTIES
www.youthspecialties.com

IDEAS LIBRARY
Ideas Library on CD-ROM 2.0
Administration, Publicity, & Fundraising
Camps, Retreats, Missions, & Service Ideas
Creative Meetings, Bible Lessons, & Worship Ideas
Crowd Breakers & Mixers
Discussion & Lesson Starters
Discussion & Lesson Starters 2
Drama, Skits, & Sketches
Drama, Skits, & Sketches 2
Drama, Skits, & Sketches 3
Games
Games 2
Games 3
Holiday Ideas
Special Events

BIBLE CURRICULA
Backstage Pass to the Bible Kit
Creative Bible Lessons from the Old Testament
Creative Bible Lessons in 1 & 2 Corinthians
Creative Bible Lessons in Galatians and Philippians
Creative Bible Lessons in John
Creative Bible Lessons in Romans
Creative Bible Lessons on the Life of Christ
Creative Bible Lessons on the Prophets
Creative Bible Lessons in Psalms
Wild Truth Bible Lessons
Wild Truth Bible Lessons 2
Wild Truth Bible Lessons—Pictures of God
Wild Truth Bible Lessons—Pictures of God 2
Wild Truth Bible Lessons—Dares from Jesus

TOPICAL CURRICULA
Creative Junior High Programs from A to Z, Vol. 1 (A-M)
Creative Junior High Programs from A to Z, Vol. 2 (N-Z)
Girls: 10 Gutsy, God-Centered Sessions on Issues That Matter to Girls
Guys: 10 Fearless, Faith-Focused Sessions on Issues That Matter to Guys
Good Sex
The Justice Mission
Live the Life! Student Evangelism Training Kit
The Next Level Youth Leader's Kit
Roaring Lambs
So What Am I Gonna Do with My Life?
Student Leadership Training Manual
Student Underground
Talking the Walk
What Would Jesus Do? Youth Leader's Kit
Wild Truth Bible Lessons
Wild Truth Bible Lessons 2
Wild Truth Bible Lessons—Pictures of God
Wild Truth Bible Lessons—Pictures of God 2
Wild Truth Bible Lessons—Dares from Jesus

DISCUSSION STARTERS

Discussion & Lesson Starters (Ideas Library)
Discussion & Lesson Starters 2 (Ideas Library)
EdgeTV
Every Picture Tells a Story
Get 'Em Talking
Keep 'Em Talking!
Good Sex Drama
Have You Ever...?
Name Your Favorite
Unfinished Sentences
What If...?
Would You Rather...?
High School TalkSheets—Updated!
More High School TalkSheets—Updated!
High School TalkSheets from Psalms and Proverbs—Updated!
Junior High-Middle School TalkSheets—Updated!
More Junior High-Middle School TalkSheets—Updated!
Junior High-Middle School TalkSheets from Psalms and Proverbs—Updated!
Real Kids Ultimate Discussion-Starting Videos:
>Castaways
>Growing Up Fast
>Hardship & Healing
>Quick Takes
>Survivors
>Word on the Street
Small Group Qs

DRAMA RESOURCES

Drama, Skits, & Sketches (Ideas Library)
Drama, Skits, & Sketches 2 (Ideas Library)
Drama, Skits, & Sketches 3 (Ideas Library)
Dramatic Pauses
Good Sex Drama
Spontaneous Melodramas
Spontaneous Melodramas 2
Super Sketches for Youth Ministry

GAME RESOURCES

Games (Ideas Library)
Games 2 (Ideas Library)
Games 3 (Ideas Library)
Junior High Game Nights
More Junior High Game Nights
Play It!
Screen Play CD-ROM

ADDITIONAL PROGRAMMING RESOURCES

(also see Discussion Starters)
The Book of Uncommon Prayers
Camps, Retreats, Missions, & Service Ideas (Ideas Library)
Creative Meetings, Bible Lessons, & Worship Ideas (Ideas Library)
Crowd Breakers & Mixers (Ideas Library)
Everyday Object Lessons

ADDITIONAL PROGRAMMING RESOURCES (con't)

Great Fundraising Ideas for Youth Groups
More Great Fundraising Ideas for Youth Groups
Great Retreats for Youth Groups
Great Talk Outlines for Youth Ministry
Holiday Ideas (Ideas Library)
Incredible Questionnaires for Youth Ministry
Kickstarters
Memory Makers
Special Events (Ideas Library)
Videos That Teach
Videos That Teach 2
Worship Services for Youth Groups

QUICK QUESTION BOOKS

Have You Ever...?
Name Your Favorite
Unfinished Sentences
What If...?
Would You Rather...?

VIDEOS & VIDEO CURRICULA

Dynamic Communicators Workshop
EdgeTV
The Justice Mission
Live the Life! Student Evangelism Training Kit
Make 'Em Laugh!
Purpose-Driven® Youth Ministry Training Kit
Real Kids Ultimate Discussion-Starting Videos:
       Castaways
       Growing Up Fast
       Hardship & Healing
       Quick Takes
       Survivors
       Word on the Street
Student Underground
Understanding Your Teenager Video Curriculum
Youth Ministry Outside the Lines

ESPECIALLY FOR JUNIOR HIGH

Creative Junior High Programs from A to Z, Vol. 1 (A-M)
Creative Junior High Programs from A to Z, Vol. 2 (N-Z)
Junior High Game Nights
More Junior High Game Nights
Junior High-Middle School TalkSheets—Updated!
More Junior High-Middle School TalkSheets—Updated!
Junior High-Middle School TalkSheets from Psalms and Proverbs—Updated!
Wild Truth Journal for Junior Highers
Wild Truth Bible Lessons
Wild Truth Bible Lessons 2
Wild Truth Journal—Pictures of God
Wild Truth Bible Lessons—Pictures of God
Wild Truth Bible Lessons—Dares from Jesus
Wild Truth Journal—Dares from Jesus

STUDENT RESOURCES
Backstage Pass to the Bible: An All-Access Tour of the New Testament
Backstage Pass to the Bible: An All-Access Tour of the Old Testament
Grow for It! Journal through the Scriptures
So What Am I Gonna Do with My Life?
Spiritual Challenge Journal: The Next Level
Teen Devotional Bible
What (Almost) Nobody Will Tell You about Sex
What Would Jesus Do? Spiritual Challenge Journal

CLIP ART
Youth Group Activities (print)
Clip Art Library Version 2.0 (CD-ROM)

DIGITAL RESOURCES
Clip Art Library Version 2.0 (CD-ROM)
Great Talk Outlines for Youth Ministry
Hot Illustrations CD-ROM
Ideas Library on CD-ROM 2.0
Screen Play
Youth Ministry Management Tools

PROFESSIONAL RESOURCES
Administration, Publicity, & Fundraising (Ideas Library)
Dynamic Communicators Workshop
Great Talk Outlines for Youth Ministry
Help! I'm a Junior High Youth Worker!
Help! I'm a Small Church Youth Worker!
Help! I'm a Small-Group Leader!
Help! I'm a Sunday School Teacher!
Help! I'm an Urban Youth Worker!
Help! I'm a Volunteer Youth Worker!
Hot Illustrations for Youth Talks
More Hot Illustrations for Youth Talks
Still More Hot Illustrations for Youth Talks
Hot Illustrations for Youth Talks 4
How to Expand Your Youth Ministry
How to Speak to Youth...and Keep Them Awake at the Same Time
Junior High Ministry (Updated & Expanded)
Just Shoot Me
Make 'Em Laugh!
The Ministry of Nurture
Postmodern Youth Ministry
Purpose-Driven® Youth Ministry
Purpose-Driven® Youth Ministry Training Kit
So That's Why I Keep Doing This!
Teaching the Bible Creatively
Your First Two Years in Youth Ministry
A Youth Ministry Crash Course
Youth Ministry Management Tools
The Youth Worker's Handbook to Family Ministry

ACADEMIC RESOURCES
Four Views of Youth Ministry & the Church
Starting Right
Youth Ministry That Transforms